HONDA SHOP MANUAL and HANDBOOK

Sport Cub Model C 110

ANNOUNCEMENT

We are happy to reproduce this Shop and Service Manual covering the extremely popular Sport Cub Model C110.

As publishers of over 200 books on automobiles and motorcycles, we have had an ever-increasing demand for shop manuals and handbooks covering Honda models, and we are therefore most happy to be able to supply these books to our customers — who consist of dealers, individuals, booksellers newsstands, riders, enthusiasts and collectors.

These books were originally printed in Japan and translated in that country. There are some expressions that differ from our own but we have left the wording exactly as it appears in the original books.

Floyd Clymer

FLOYD CLYMER PUBLICATIONS
World's Largest Publisher of Books Relating to Automobiles, Motorcycles, Motor Racing, and Americana
222 NO. VIRGIL AVENUE AT BEVERLY BLVD., LOS ANGELES 4, CALIFORNIA

INTRODUCTION

Welcome to the world of digital publishing ~ the book you now hold in your hand, while unchanged from the original **1970** edition, was printed using the latest state of the art digital technology. The advent of print-on-demand has forever changed the publishing process, never has information been so accessible and it is our hope that this book serves your informational needs for years to come. If this is your first exposure to digital publishing, we hope that you are pleased with the results. Many more titles of interest to the classic automobile and motorcycle enthusiast, collector and restorer are available via our website at **www.VelocePress.com.** We hope that you find this title as interesting as we do.

NOTE FROM THE PUBLISHER

The information presented is true and complete to the best of our knowledge. All recommendations are made without any guarantees on the part of the author or the publisher, who also disclaim all liability incurred with the use of this information.

TRADEMARKS

We recognize that some words, model names and designations, for example, mentioned herein are the property of the trademark holder. We use them for identification purposes only. This is not an official publication.

INFORMATION ON THE USE OF THIS PUBLICATION

This manual is an invaluable resource for the classic **HONDA** enthusiast and a "must have" for owners interested in performing their own maintenance. However, in today's information age we are constantly subject to changes in common practice, new technology, availability of improved materials and increased awareness of chemical toxicity. As such, it is advised that the user consult with an experienced professional prior to undertaking any procedure described herein. While every care has been taken to ensure correctness of information, it is obviously not possible to guarantee complete freedom from errors or omissions or to accept liability arising from such errors or omissions. Therefore, any individual that uses the information contained within, or elects to perform or participate in do-it-yourself repairs or modifications acknowledges that there is a risk factor involved and that the publisher or its associates cannot be held responsible for personal injury or property damage resulting from the use of the information or the outcome of such procedures.

It is important that the reader recognizes that any instructions may refer to either the right-hand or left-hand sides of the vehicle or the components and that the directions are followed carefully. One final word of advice, this publication is intended to be used as a reference guide, and when in doubt the reader should consult with a qualified technician.

HONDA SHOP MANUAL & HANDBOOK

Sport Cub Model C 110

INTRODUCTION

This manual is designed as a service handbook for the C-110 Honda "50". By carefully reading this manual, the service man will be able to perform a thorough service and the salesman can gain a working knowledge of the machine.

This manual has 4 chapters, each is separated into sections. The sections are broken down into the following sequence — Disassembling, Inspection, Service and Assembling.

Provisions have been made for service memorandum at the end of each chapter. Please keep track of design modifications or special notes -- If you write it down here you won't forget.

An effort has been made to produce a manual avoiding fundamental principle and theory by explaining the actual mechanism. Special emphasis has been placed on illustrations and charts to make it easy for the service man to understand without reading every line.

Please remember the service department at American Honda Motor Co. is here to serve you. Feel free to call upon us at any time.

Sincerely,

American Honda Motor Co., Inc.

Service Department

INDEX

		Page
I REMOVING ENGINE FROM FRAME		1
I-1	Cylinder Head Cover	1
I-2	Cylinder Head	1
I-3	Cam Timing & Valves	2
I-4	Cylinder Piston & Piston Rings	4
I-5	Crankshaft & Connecting Rod	5
I-6	Crankcase	7
I-7	Lubrication	8
I-8	Transmission	9
I-9	Clutch	10
I-10	Carburetor	10
II FRAME		
II-1	Handlebars Wire & Cables	12
II-2	Front Fork	12
II-3	Front Suspension	13
II-4	Rear Suspension	14
II-5	Drive Chain	15
II-6	Front Wheel & Rear Wheel	16
	Tires	17
II-7	Brakes	18
II-8	Fuel Tank & Seat	19
II-9	Air Cleaner	19
II-10	Exhaust System	19
II-11	Peg Bar Center Stand & Brake Pedal	19
II-12	Frame	20
III ELECTRICAL SYSTEM		
III-1	Ignition System	22
	Condenser	23
	Flywheel Magneto	24
	Ignition Coil	24
III-2	Charging System	25
	Rectifier	26
	Battery	26
	Specific Gravity Value	27

		Page
III-3	Switches	28
III-4	Electrical loads & Speedometer	30
	Horn	30
	Directional Signal Light Relay	30
	Speedometer	31
	Headlamp	31
	Tail Lamp & Speedometer Lamp	31
	Directional Signal Lamp	32
	Fuse	32
	Wiring Harness	32

IV INSPECTION, MAINTENANCE & SPECIFICATION

IV-1	Preventative Maintenance	35
	Engine Tune-up	35
	Tappet Adjustment	36
	Ignition Timing	37
	Spark Plugs	38
	Ignition Coil	38
	Condensor Test	38
	Fuel Supply	38
	Cleaning & Adjustment of Carburetor	39
	Adjustment of Drive Chain	40
	Adjusting Brakes	41
	Battery Care	41-42
	Lubrication	42-43
	Drive Chain Lubrication	43
	Inspection for Tightening of Various Parts	43
	Torque Values	44
	Tightening of Spokes	45
IV-2	Periodical Inspection & Maintenance	45
	Daily Inspection	45
	Periodical Inspection Chart	46
IV-3	Diagnosis of Troubles	47-55
IV-4	Maintenance Data & Specifications	56
	Specification of Parts	57-59
	Wiring Diagram	60

I. ENGINE

REMOVING ENGINE FROM FRAME

Disconnect and remove battery at clips
Remove electric wire connectors involved
Exhaust pipe and muffler (will come off in one unit)
Left crankcase cover
Drive chain joint
Foot peg bar
Inlet pipe connecting tube
Upper rear engine mount bolt
Lower rear engine mount bolt

MOUNTING THE ENGINE IN FRAME

Reverse the above procedure. Please be careful not to pinch the battery vent tube or wires.

1-1 CYLINDER HEAD COVER

    A Disassembly
        (1) Loosen the 4-head cover nuts (6m/n) and the oil joint bolt
        (2) Check the surface for warpage. If there is more than 0.05 mm be sure to resurface
    B Assembly
        (1) Use new packing. Be sure to assemble the rocker arms before installing the head cover
        (2) Before you tighten the cover make sure the push rods are in the rocker arm socket—torque nuts to 5 foot lbs. using X pattern shown in fig. 2.
        (3) Be sure to check the tappet adjustment after assembly

1-2 CYLINDER HEAD

    A Disassembly
        (1) Remove the head cover following #1-1
        (2) Be sure to check for oil leaks, compression leak, and scratches while you are disassembling.

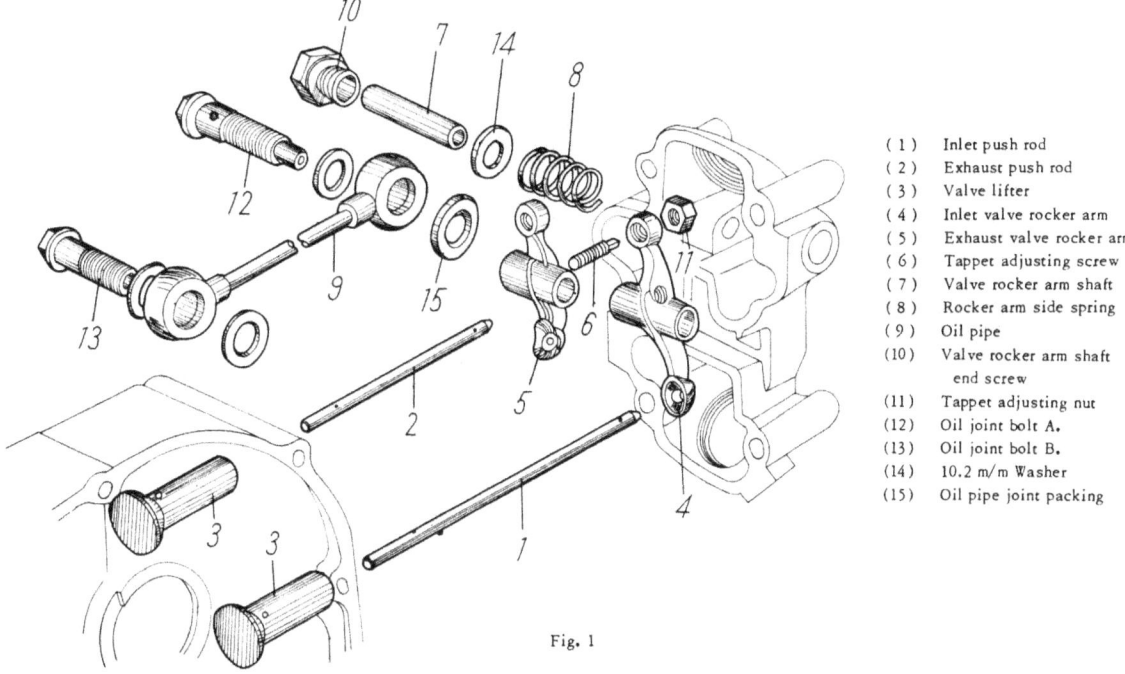

(1) Inlet push rod
(2) Exhaust push rod
(3) Valve lifter
(4) Inlet valve rocker arm
(5) Exhaust valve rocker arm
(6) Tappet adjusting screw
(7) Valve rocker arm shaft
(8) Rocker arm side spring
(9) Oil pipe
(10) Valve rocker arm shaft end screw
(11) Tappet adjusting nut
(12) Oil joint bolt A.
(13) Oil joint bolt B.
(14) 10.2 m/m Washer
(15) Oil pipe joint packing

Fig. 1

B Assembly Inspection
(1) First, check the cylinder head gasket for leaks. Then clean the carbon in the combustion chamber. Be careful not to scratch the combustion chamber or piston crown.
(2) If you noticed any gasket leaks check the head for warp. Resurface if necessary.
(3) In assembling the cylinder head, use new "o" rings & gaskets. Don't forget the "o" rings. The long push rod is the intake and goes on the right side.
(4) When tightening the cylinder stud nuts, follow the direction of fig. 2. Use a torque wrench—torque to 5 ft.-lbs.

Fig. 2
Tightening Order of Cylinder Head

1-3 CAM TIMING AND VALVES

A Disassembly of Rocker Arms
(1) Remove the rocker shaft bolts and pull out the rocker arms, see figure 1.

B Inspection
(1) Check for wear of the push rod socket and the tappet adjusting screw.
(2) Check the diameter of the rocker arm shafts and the inside diameter of the rocker arms. If they are worn, replace.
(3) Check rocker arm end play, it should be 0.6mm-1.0mm (.025"-.040") if the clearance exceeds the limit, replace the 10.2mm washer.

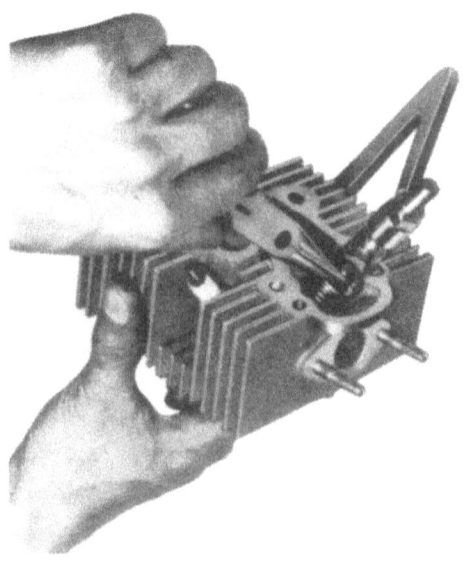

Fig. 3

Fig. 4

(4) Check the push rods for straightness; if they are bent more than 0.5mm (.020") replace.

C Valve Lifter Disassembly and Inspection
  (1) After removing the cam shaft, direction 1-3 remove the valve lifters.
  (2) Check for wear of the valve lifter face, replace if necessary.
  (3) Check the outer diameter of the valve lifter shaft for wear.
  (4) Check valve lifter guides in crankcase for wear.

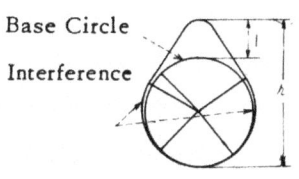

Fig. 5

CAM PROFILE

D Cam Shaft Disassembly
  (1) Remove the right side crank case cover.
  (2) Remove the oil guide, bend the clutch nut lock back and loosen the clutch nut, pull the clutch off the shaft.
  (3) Remove the 14mm circlip and pull the primary driven gear off of of the shaft.
  (4) Remove the oil strainer and pull the cam shaft from the case.
  (5) If cam is to be removed while the cylinder head is still on the engine, slack off on the valve adjustment.

E Inspection
  (1) Measure the cam lobe height, if it is less than .906" replace cam shaft.
  (2) Check cam shaft bearings in case for wear.
  (3) Check timing gears for wear.
  (4) The cam gear bolt should be tightened to 11-13 ft.-lb of torque.
  (5) Be sure to match the timing marks when reassembling cam shaft to the engine, see figure 4.

F Valve Disassembly
  (1) Use valve spring compressor provided in the special tool kit. See fig. 3.

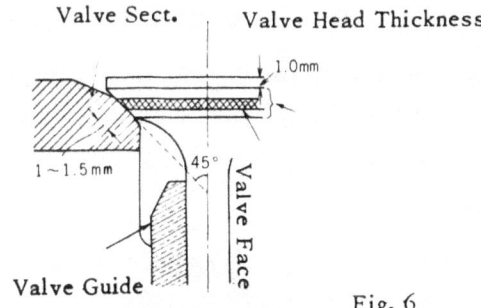

Fig. 6

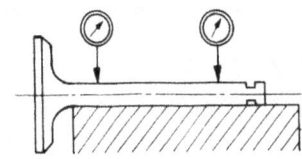

Checking Bent of Valve Stem by Dial Gage

Fig. 7

G Valve Inspection
  (1) Clean the valves with a wire wheel, check for burning or pitting, thickness of the valve head must not be less than 0.2mm (.008") for the intake and 0.4mm (.016") for the exhaust. See figure 6.
  (2) Check the valve stem for excessive wear.
  (3) If the valve stem is excessively worn and needs replacement, the valve guide will be worn also and the new valve will not seat properly. To replace the valve guide, heat the head to 300 degrees C', drive out the old guide and install the new guide. Make sure it is properly positioned. After the head has cooled off at room temperature, finish the inside diameter of the valve guide with the reamer provided in the special tool kit.
  (4) Check the valve stem for straightness. See figure 7.
  (5) Place the valve spring on a surface plate and measure the free height. It should be, for the outer spring, 28.4-27.8mm (1.120"-1.095"). For the inner spring, 26.9-29mm (1.060"-1.023"). Also

check spring tension. The outer spring should be compressed to 23.5 mm (925"). It should measure 18.5-20.5 pounds. The inner spring compressed to 19 mm (.748") and should measure 35.5-39 pounds.
(6) If the wear of the valve seat is mild, lap the valve in with fine valve lapping compound. If the seats are pitted or burned they will have to be repaired with the valve seat cutters provided in the special tool kit. First clean up the seat with the 45° angle cutter and then clean up the seat with the 120° and 30° cutters according to figure 6. Remove a minimum of metal. If too much is removed, the head will have to be replaced.
(7) Lap the valve with fine compound, clean the valve and seat thoroughly. Oil the valve stem for assembly.

1-4 CYLINDER, PISTON AND PISTON RING

A Disassemble, Inspection, Assemble
(1) Follow instructions for cylinder head removal.
(2) Measure the cylinder bore by a suitable guage. If over the maximum limit rebore to next oversize. American Honda Motor Co. recommends the use of a hone after boring. You should leave 0.02 mm for honing after boring. If you are going to replace only the piston, recondition the out-of-round part by ridge reamer. The tolerance of recondition must be within 0 to 0.01 mm; taper must not be in excess of 0.01 mm.
(3) Install rings with gap every 120° avoiding piston thrust face. Be careful not to damage the rings.

B Disassemble, Inspection
(1) Remove piston by removing piston pin clip and piston pin. Be care-careful not to loose the clip in the crankcase.
(2) Remove the rings by your thumb or special tool. Be sure not to warp them.
(3) Remove the carbon on top of the piston and in grooves. Wash them (clean). Do not use sandpaper.
(4) Check the piston and replace it when it is necessary. Measure the piston by micrometer at right angle to the piston pin and skirt. Perform amends whenever necessary according to specifications.

Fig. 8

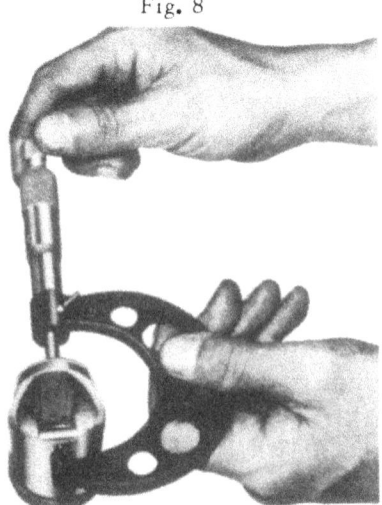

Measuring Diameter of Piston Skirt

Fig. 9

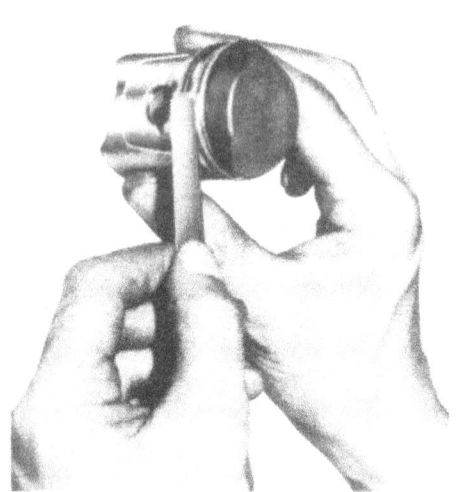

Checking Clearance Between Piston Ring Groove and Ring

(5) Clearance of groove must be measured by fitting new rings and perform repairs according to the specifications if necessary.

(6) Measure the piston pin hole with a hole gauge and perform the necessary repairs according to the specifications. Fig. 10.
(7) Oversize pistons are available in three different sizes: STD. 0.25 mm, 0.50 mm and 0.75 mm.
(8) When replacing the piston, be sure to place the mark "F" to the machines front. If you are going to use oversize piston and rings, use the right cylinder barrel for them. Clearance between piston and barrel is between 0 and 0.03 mm.

C Inspection and Connection of Piston
  (1) Measure the wear of diameter by micrometer and perform the necessary amend according to the specification.
  (2) Tightness between piston pin and cam rod is a lite push fit. Always use new piston pin clips.

G Inspection & Checking
  (1) Remove the rings from the piston and put them into the cylinder barrel evenly and measure the clearance of the gap by thickness gauge and if the clearance exceeds 1.00 mm replace the ring. Fig. 11.
  (2) Always check old rings for tension. Compare them with new rings. Thickness must be measured by thickness gauge. Perform the repairs needed.
  (3) Before assembling the ring, place in barrel and check the gap clearance to 0.1 - 0.3 mm. If too small, file end of ring lightly.
  (4) Be sure not to place the rings on piston with face down. The rings are marked 'top' - top goes towards top of piston.

1-5 CRANK SHAFT & CONNECTING ROD

A Disassemble
  (1) Drain the crankcase oil.
  (2) Remove the head cover, cylinder head and cylinder.
  (3) Remove the right crankcase cover and remove clutch compt., gear shift spindle compt., and cam shaft. Pull out the timing gear.
  (4) Remove the flywheel magneto and coil on left side.
  (5) Loosen the nine (9) bolts and separate the crankcase, while carefully pressing the drum stopper downward.
  (6) Remove the crankshaft.

B Inspection & Connection
  (1) Support main bearings on "V" blocks and place the dial gauges to read the free play. If out of specifications, repair.

Fig. 10

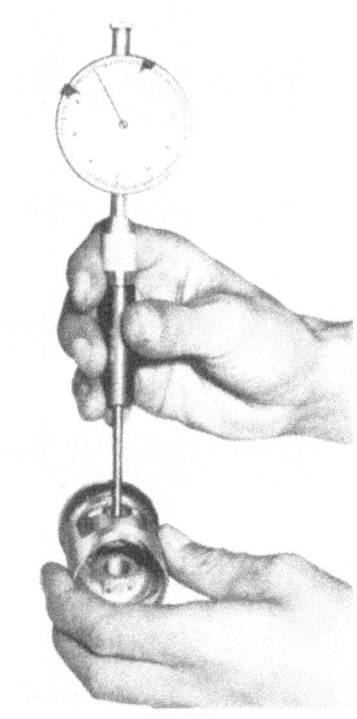

Fig. 11
Measuring Piston Ring End Gap

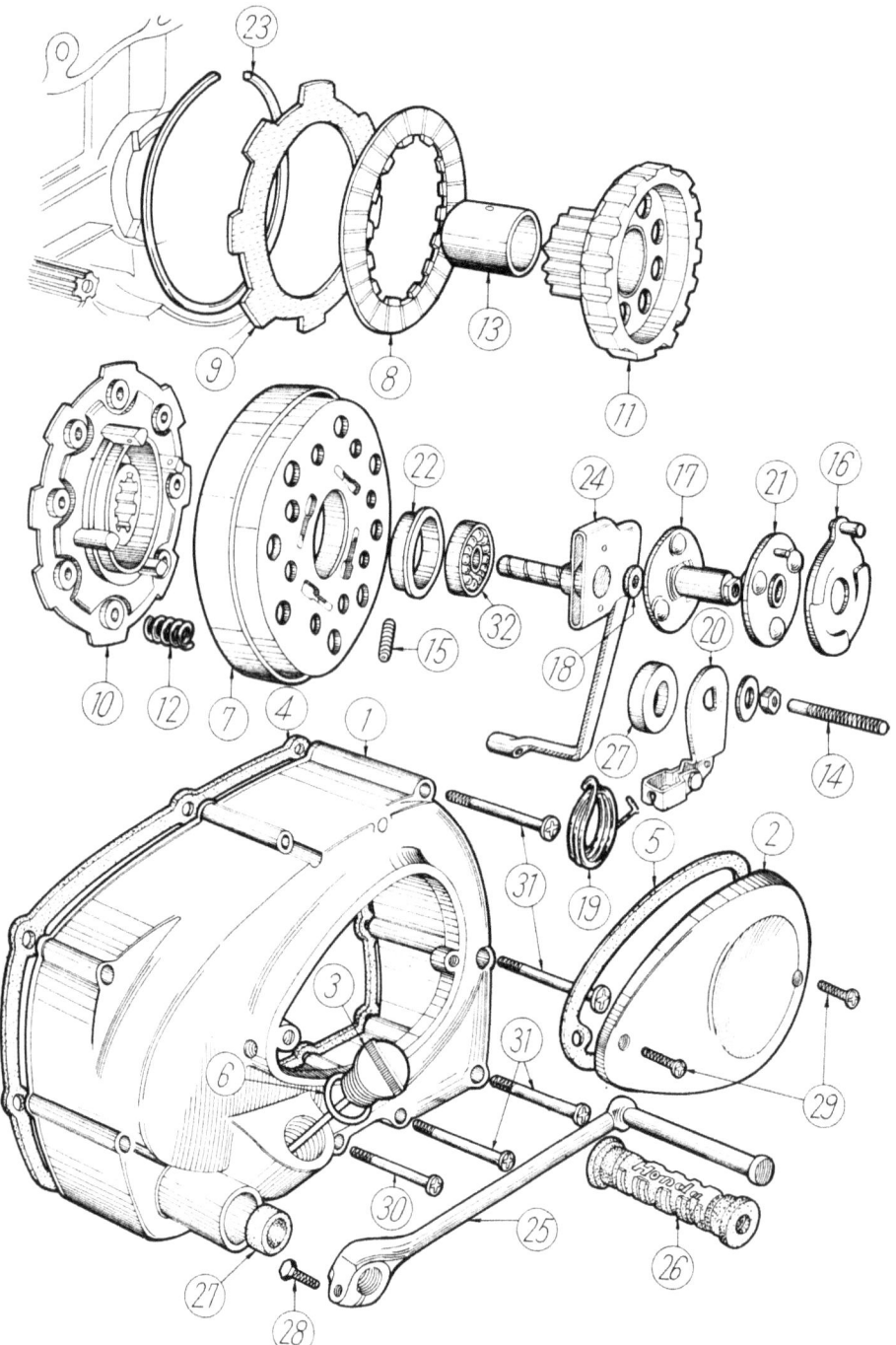

(1) R. crank case cover
(2) Clutch cover
(3) Oil gage comp.
(4) R crank case cover packing
(5) Clutch cover packing
(6) Oil cap packing
(7) Clutch outer
(8) Clutch friction disk
(9) Clutch plate
(10) Drive plate comp.
(11) Drive gear
(12) Clutch spring
(13) Clutch center guide
(14) Clutch lift adjusting screw
(15) Clutch damper spring
(16) Clutch cam plate comp.
(17) Clutch lifter comp.
(18) 4.3 m m/ 0 ring
(19) Clutch lever spring
(20) Clutch lever comp.
(21) Clutch ball retainer comp.
(22) Bearing shell
(23) 101 mm Set ring
(24) Oil guide comp.
(25) Kick starter arm
(26) Kick starter rubber
(27) S 11.62410 Oil seal
(28) 6 x 20 Hex. bolt
(29) 6 x 16 Cross Rec. screw
(30) 6 x 40 Cross Rec. screw
(31) 6 x 60 Cross Rec. screw
(32) 6000 x Ball bearing

(2) Place the balance weight on the block and put the dial gauge on the bearing outer race and measure the amount of free play by moving the outer race up and down. Perform repairs according to specifications if necessary.

(3) Assembling crankshaft must be done by special tools in a hydraulic press using 4 tons of pressure. Fig. 13.

C Connecting Rod Inspection

(1) Measure the inner diameter of small end and perform the amend if necessary according to the specifications.

(2) Place the crankshaft on "V" blocks and measure the free play of the rod's big end by the dial guage. Make sure it is within specifications. Fig. 14.

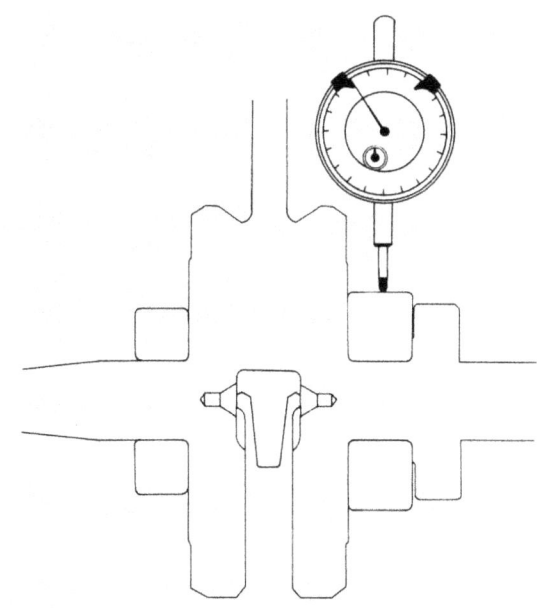

Fig. 12
Checking Radial Clearance of Crank Shaft Bearing

(3) Replace the crankshaft if the swing span of small end is in excess of 3.00 mm.

(4) Total amount of distortion consisting of bending, twisting and uneven defacement of the connecting rod is measured by the amount of discrepancy between both ends of a 80mm push fit bar inserted in the small end of the connecting rod, when it is swung as in the paragraph above.

Fig. 13
Pressing Crank Shaft

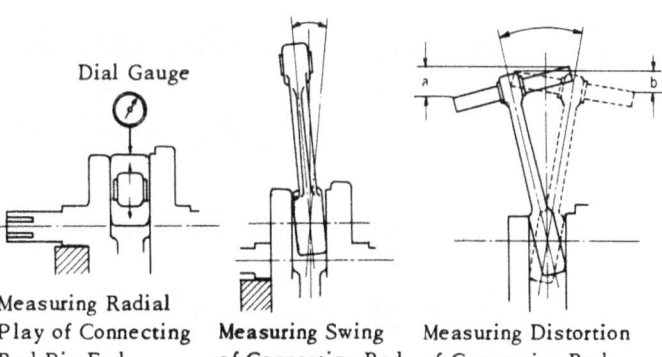

Fig. 14

1-6 CRANKCASE

A Disassemble

(1) Drain the crankcase oil.
(2) Remove the head cover, cylinder head and cylinder.
(3) Loosen the nine (9) screws which hold on the right crankcase cover. Remove the right crankcase cover.
(4) Straighten the 14 mm lock washer and remove the 14 mm nut. Remove the clutch-complete.

(5) Remove the 17 mm circle clip and remove the primary driven gear.
(6) Remove the kick starter spring.
(7) Remove the camshaft.
(8) Remove the flywheel.
(9) Remove the starter assembly.
(10) Loosen (remove) the two bolts on the drive sprocket and remove same.
(11) Remove the nine (9) screws which tighten the crankcase and separate the crankcase.
(12) After splitting the crankcase take out the transmission gears.
(13) Crankshaft can be removed from case by removing the timing gears with timing gear puller from special tool kit.

1-7 LUBRICATION

A Lubrication of the C110 "Sports Cub"

The C110 is wet sump and although simple in design it is very efficient. Oil is distributed to the crankshaft from the oil sump by the cam gear and dipper on the big end of the rod which splashes oil to the piston and cylinder walls. See Fig. 16.

Oil is also forced through the screw type groove machined in the camshaft. This pumps oil up to the rocker arms. The oil then returns to the sump through a drillway in the cylinder.

On the later C110, the rocker arm oil feed pipe is routed through the carburator, to act as a heat riser.

Transmission and clutch are taken care of by splash from the crankshaft and cam gear.

To check oiling just loosen oil feed pipe joint bolt at the head. Run the engine at half speed and check flow of oil. See Fig. 17 for Lubrication diagram.

Fig. 18
Removing Fly-Wheel Nut

B Inspection, Assembly
(1) Check the surface of the sealing edges of the crankcase and crankcase covers. Use new gaskets always. Gaskets don't cost much and it may save you from doing a job over.
(2) Assemble transmission and crankshaft before hand into the Left crankcase cover.

Fig. 16

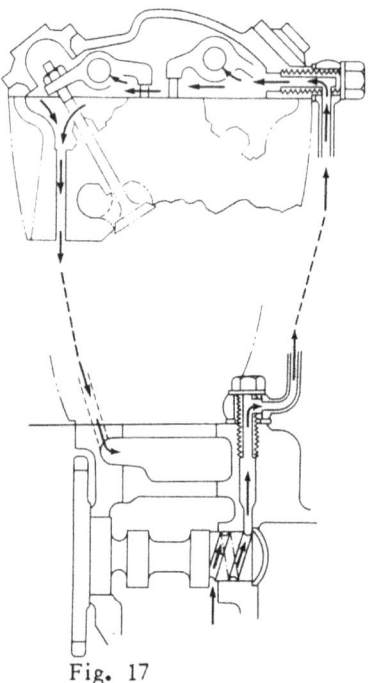

Fig. 17

1-8 TRANSMISSION

A Disassemble, Inspection and Service
(1) Remove Left Side Cover—
(a) Remove the fly wheel nut by holding the fly wheel firmly with the holder and puller both supplied to you in your tool kit. See Fig. 18. Note: Do not hit or force it off with a hammer as you may bend the shaft.
(b) Starter can be removed by removing two 6 mm flat head screws. Be sure to disconnect the high tension cord and neutral switch cord.

B Drive sprocket can be removed by removing the two 6 mm bolts and fixing plate. You will find a sprocket holder in your Honda tool kit. See Fig. 19.

(2) Remove Right Side Cover—
(a) Remove the kick starter arm and tighten screws to separate the cover.
(b) Remove the oil trough and straighten the 14 mm lock washers. Remove the 14 mm locknut to take off the clutch.
(c) Remove the driver gear by taking off the 17 mm circle crip.
(d) If the shift mechanism is to be removed, check if shift drum is in the center of the shift arm claws or not. (It should be in the center of both claws.) If not, it will make it difficult to shift. Also check the wear of the drum pin, movement of drum, tension of spring, straightness of stopper and return spring pin. Check the nuts and bolts for tightness.
(e) After checking the parts mentioned above, remove them.
(f) Remove the 23 mm circle clip and take off the kick starter spring.
(g) Remove the nine screws which hold the crankcase and lay the engine's Right crankcase up; remove the Right case.

Fig. 19
Removing Drive Sprocket Clamp Bolt

(h) Check these items:— wear of teeth, free play, wear of spline, outer diameter of shaft, inner diameter of gears, wear of bearings, wear of starter shaft, wear of shaft spring. Perform the services necessary according to the specification.
(i) Drum can be removed by loosening the 6 mm bolt which is on the Left crankcase inside of the 19mm rubber plug.
(j) Remove the shift fork by straightening the shift fork pin lock washer and removing the guide pin. Check the wear of shift fork, uneven wear, wear of the groove or the drum, or the outer diameter of drum.

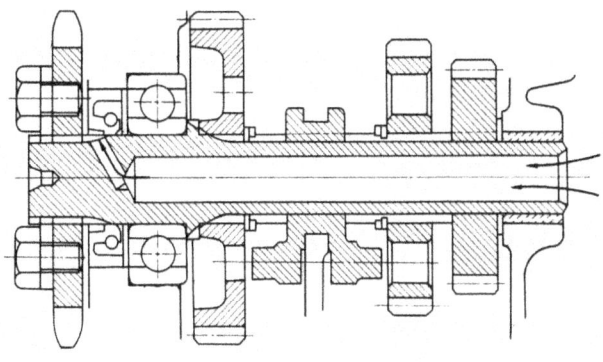

Fig. 20
Breather

C Breather
The breather of the "Sports Cub" is placed in counter shaft, which is shown in Fig. 20.

1-9   CLUTCH

   A   Disassembly
   (1) Right cover is removed by removing nine screws which hold it on.
   (2) Take off the oil trough, ball bearing, bearing shell, straighten the 14 mm lock washer and remove the lock nut. Then remove the clutch comp.
   (3) In order to disassemble the clutch-complete, one has to hold and compress the clutch outer and drive plate by using a tool, found in the '50' kit, drill press or vise to release the 101 mm set ring. Remove the set ring and disassemble the clutch. Be careful not to damage the part where the vise holds. Use a cloth or wood in order not to damage the clutch. Do the same when you re-assemble it.
   (4) Clutch cam plate and ball retainer can be removed by removing the 6 mm clutch lever screws on right crankcase.

   B   Inspection, Service
   (1) Usually clutch adjustment can be done either by cable adjuster or by removing the clutch cover. Loosen 6 mm nut and adjust screw to just touching. If this doesn't work, check the clutch-complete.
   (2) Check whether clutch left adjust screw is pushing on center of oil trough. If not, find out why and replace parts if necessary.
   (3) Check the wear of the clutch release ball bearing.
   (4) Check the clearance between crank shaft and clutch center guide, drive gear and guides. Repair or replace if necessary.
   (5) Check the wear of the teeth on clutch plate, wear in thickness, and warp. Repair or replace if needed.
   (6) Check the wear of clutch friction disk teeth, wear in thickness, and warp. Repair or replace if needed. (Fig. 21).
   (7) Check the clutch spring for tension.
   (8) Check the teeth of drive gear for wear. Replace if needed.
   (9) If the wear of teeth on driven gear is excessive it should be changed. Worn gears are noisy. Changing them keeps dealer from doing job over.
   (10) Check the wear of clutch cam plate, clutch lifter plate (especially where the balls are attached) and replace them when wear is excessive.
   (11) Check the wear of ball retainer.

1-10   CARBURETOR

   A   Adjustments

   The carburetor must be adjusted to run the engine at its best. It also must be adjusted to produce the same ratio of gas and air from idling to maximum revolutions—and it must be kept cool at this maximum. If it is too 'lean' at top speed it will create heat and ruin the engine.

   The carburetor is made to perform the above duties. Many parts are made with special care for long life. The jet needle, needle jet, throttle valve, float valve are parts which move all the time so they are made to endure the long use by using special materials and fine surface finishes.

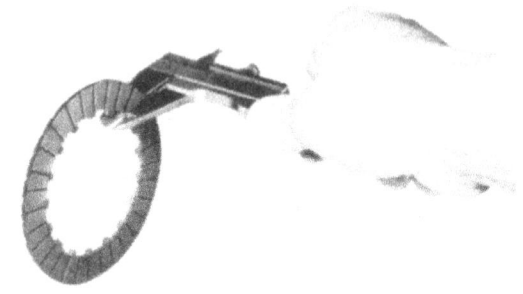

Fig. 21
Measuring Friction Disk Thickness

   It is not desirable to change the settings without checking with the carburetor manufacturer or our specifications, so if you are going to change

the adjustment or have to repair the carburetor, be sure you do as follows:-
   (1) It must be adjusted to meet the needs of the engine at all speeds.
   (2) Check for air leaks at the carburetor mounting points.
   (3) Always use new packings and "O" rings when repairing carburetor.

D Adjustment at high speed
   (1) When running at full throttle if the speed becomes faster when you close the choke, this shows that the mixture is lean—change the main jet to the next larger size. (Main jets are made in steps of 5's ie, 100, 105, 110 etc.
   (2) If you close the choke and the speed is reduced this shows the mixture is accurate or too rich.
      (a) Mixture is accurate—if you put in the next smaller main jet and the speed becomes slower. If the speed becomes faster by closing the choke this means the former jet was accurate and that the present one is too small.
      (b) If the mixture is too lean—do not run the engine until you richen it back up—don't forget that heat is the greatest enemy to an air-cooled engine. Nothing will produce heat like a lean mixture.

E Adjustment at Middle Speed
   (1) Jet Needle—
      (a) There are black exhaust gas fumes from the engine at middle speed. This phenomenon shows mixture is too rich, lower the needle.
      (b) If there is engine miss while you accelerate, raise the needle.
   (2) Cut away of throttle Valve—
      You can get the richer throttle cutaway by the large number and the smaller you can get the leaner.

F Adjustment at low speed.
   Mixture at the throttle opening from idling to 1/8 must be done by air screw and throttle valve cutaway.
   (1) Air Screw—
      Mixture adjustment at idling must be done by the air screw. To richen turn in the screw—back out to lean. This air screw adjustment must be done not only for the idling but also for the point of the throttle opening just above idling.
   (2) Cutaway—
      Sometimes one can't adjust the mixture ratio at the 1/8 of throttle opening. In this case this can be adjusted by using a larger number cutaway if it is too lean and a smaller number if it is too rich. Then again adjust the air screw after fitting new valve.

G Adjustment of Float Level - See Fig. 22 - Page 12
   (1) Remove float cover.
   (2) Place carburetor with float hinge pin (4) on the top.
   (3) Now move float (1) in toward the main body of the carburetor until the float arm (3) is just resting on float valve (2).
   (4) Now measure the distance between (5) and (6).
   (5) It should be 19.5 mm ± .5 mm.
   (6) If you do not have this distance you can correct it by carefully bending (3) until it is right.
   (7) H = 19.5 mm (.767 ins).

II. FRAME

2-1 STEERING HANDLE (BAR), WIRES AND CABLES.

A Disassemble

Remove the throttle, clutch, front brake wire and remove the head light. Disconnect the wire connectors, allowing you to remove the four bolts which hold the bar. The bar can be removed together with these wires.

Speedometer can be removed by removing the setting spring and the speedometer cable.

Details of Removing—
(1) Front brake wire can be removed by removing the Right steering handle lever.
(2) Clutch wire can be removed by removing left steering handle lever.
(3) Throttle wire can be removed by taking off the right grip clamp (remove two screws) and release grip by twisting. Pull out the throttle wire from bar by removing throttle wire slide and outer cover stop.

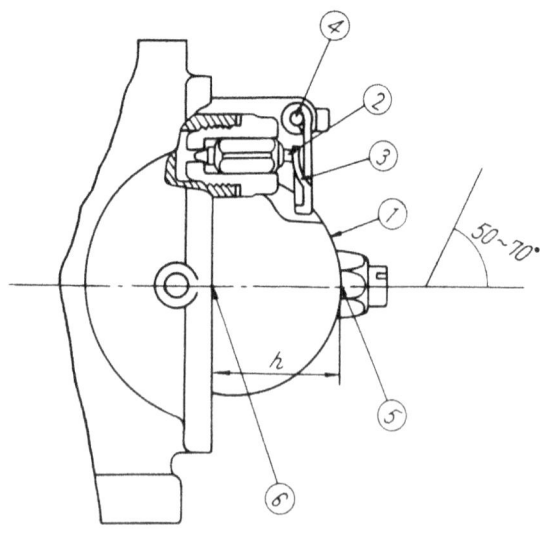

Fig. 22

B Inspection and Assembly
  (1) Any damage of outer cover of throttle wire, clutch wire, or brake wire should be fixed by tape or replacement.
  (2) If the wires which were mentioned above were damaged and affect the movement of the inner wire, replace them.
  (3) Speedometer cable outer cover must be replaced when it is kinked or it will break the inner wire. Always oil the cable before reassembling. Also put grease on the throttle wire stop and throttle grip slide before assembling. Assembly must be done opposite of dissembly. The longer handle bar setting bolts are used in front.

2-2 FRONT FORK

A Disassemble.

Remove the front wheel. Then remove the steering handle bar according to the procedure of former chapter. Disconnect the horn assembly wires and winker wires. Remove the steering stem nut. Remove the 8 mm bolt which tightens fork top bridge plate. The front fork assembly can be removed by removing steering head top crown nut by using 36m/m pin spanner. Fig. 23. The headlight case can be removed by removing attached bolts (one is for ground, so be careful when disassembling). Front fender can be removed by loosening thin nuts on front shock upper mount bolt and 8m/m nuts of front arm pivot.

B Inspection
  (1) Replace the 3/16" steel balls if there is wear or damage. There are 21 balls (top and bottom, 42 total).
  (2) Check the cone race especially where balls touch and replace if there is excess or uneven wear.
  (3) Replace the front fork if you measure excess bending at fork or stem.
  (4) Replace the rubber bush of front brake torque link if there is any damage or distortion. Bushes are pressed in a press. You may use a hammer — but be careful.

C Assemble

Assemble the head light case, front fender and other parts and put the steering stem into the head pipe. Tighten the head pipe and stem with steering head nut. At first, tighten the top slightly stiff (by using 36 mm pin spanner) and tightening the bolt on the top plate. After completing the above, loosen the steering head top thread in full.

Steering must be tightened (fork) to turn easily so that the fork continues to move when given a slight touch. There must not be any free play (clearance) at the ball races.

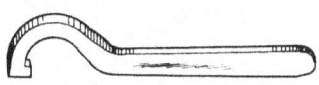

36 mm Spanner
Fig. 23

Remarks—
(1) Be sure to grease the ball races, using a fiber grease.
(2) Do not tighten the polyethylene parts too tight.

2-3 FRONT ARM & FRONT CUSHION

A Front Arm
(1) Disassemble

Remove the front wheel and the front arm pivot bolt, the front shock and the upper bolt. The front cushion and front arm can now be easily removed from fork leg. Disassemble the front suspension arm from front shock by removing lower bolt.

There are dust seal, cap, and collar in the front arm and these should be taken apart to be cleaned or replaced if needed. See Fig. 24.

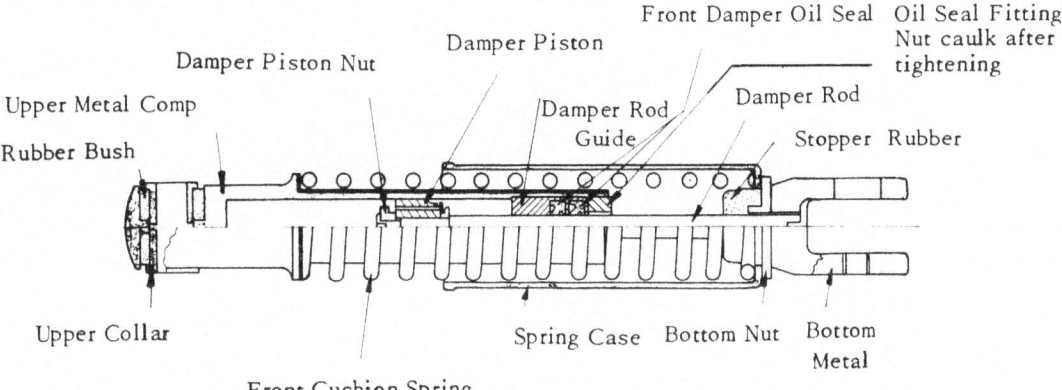

Fig. 24

(2) Inspection and Assembly
(a) If there is a big clearance between front arm pivot bolt and pivot collar, check the bolt and perform the necessary service.
(b) If there is a big clearance between pivot collar and suspension arm, replace the collar.
(c) If there is a big clearance between front cushion, lower distance collar and suspension arm, replace collar.
(d) Damaged or worn dust seals must be replaced.
(e) Distorted or damaged front arm rebound stopper rubber must be changed.

Assembling is easy but be careful; there is a "R" and "L" of the arm. Be sure to grease after assembly.

B Front Cushion (Shock)
(1) Disassemble

Disassemble by following the procedure used in Fig. 24. First, end of piston rod and bottom metal are locked by a bent washer.

Straighten the washer and hold the locknut (2) by a wrench and remove the bottom metal (1). Hold the groove on the end of the damper rod with a screw driver and remove the bottom locknut (2). Remove the spring case and spring.

During the disassembly do not hold the inside rod with any tool which might damage it, i.e. a vise or vise grips, etc.

(2) Inspection & Assembly

(a) Measure the angle, free length and tension of the spring. Replace them if it does not conform with specifications.

(b) Check for oil leaks of the shock damper and replace damper if necessary.

(c) Replace the damper if there is any scratches, bending or distortion on the rod.

(d) Replace the upper metal rubber bush when it is damaged or distorted.

After checking all parts reassembling must be done by pulling out the damper rod as far as possible and installing the spring and spring case over the rod. By compressing the spring, install the lock nut on the end of the damper rod and screw the lock nut to the end, holding the shaft with a screw driver. Install the bottom metal securely and lock the end of the rod to the bottom metal.

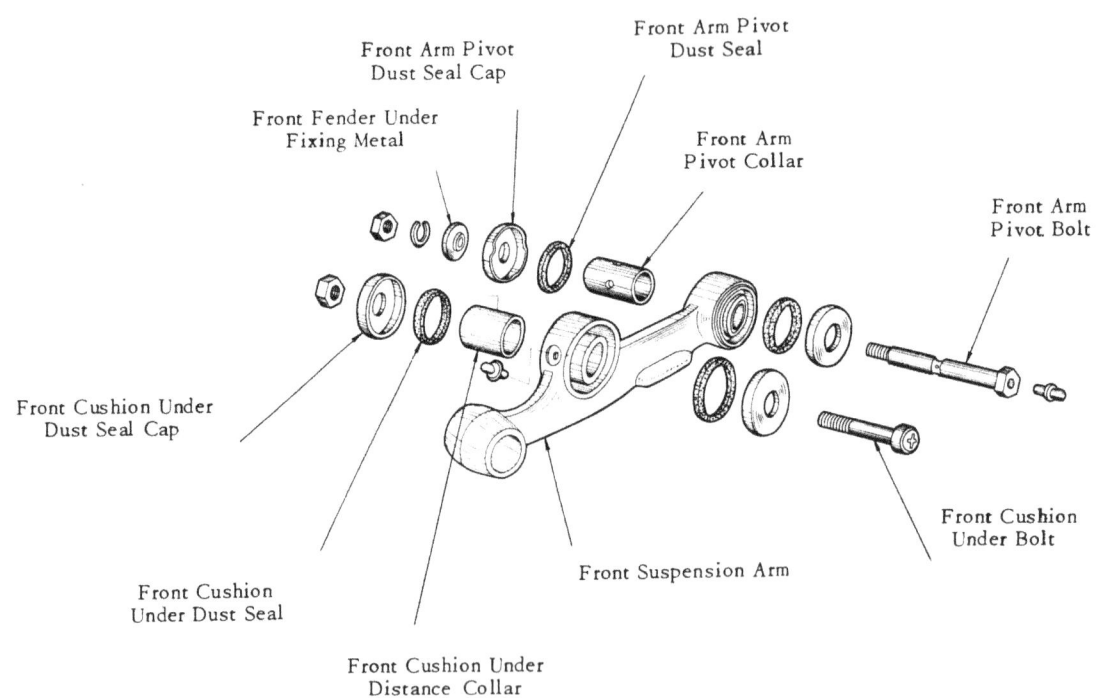

Fig. 25

2-4 REAR FORK & REAR CUSHION

A Rear Fork

(1) Disassemble

(a) Remove the upper and lower chain case and chain.

(b) Remove the rear wheel and final drive flange. Remove the rear shock bottom mount bolt and pull out the pivot bolt. The rear fork is now off.

(2) Inspection & Assemble

(a) Replace the worn and damaged drive chain case packing.

(b) Replace the rear fork pivot rubber bush if it is damaged or distorted and doesn't move smoothly. Bushes are pressed in, so replace them one by one, using the hydraulic press.

(c) Visually inspect distortion or twist and replace the rear fork if it is damaged or twisted.

(d) Replace brake torque link if the hole is enlarged. Replace the spring if it is weak.

Assemble the fork to the frame by putting in the pivot bolt and installing the nut. Tighten it with the strength of 26.75-29.6 ft.-lb. After setting this, the chain case will be ready for assembly but, be sure to put the chain case packing into the appropriate place.

B Rear Cushion

(1) Disassemble.

(a) Remove the upper metal by removing the upper lock nut after compressing the rear shock upper cover by tool or by hand.

(b) The upper cover and the rear shock spring will now come out.

(c) The spring guide and the stopper rubber may come out at the same time.

(d) DO NOT disassemble the rear damper. We do not stock the parts for it and the damper nut is locked on at the factory.

(2) Inspection & Assemble.

(a) Measure the rear cushion spring and perform the amend according to the specifications if necessary.

(b) Replace the damper assembly when the damper rod is damaged, distorted, or if there is a leak in the rod.

(c) Replace the stopper rubber when it is damaged or distorted excessively.

(d) Replace the upper and lower rubber bush when it is damaged or distorted.

Assembly can be done in the opposite procedure of disassembling. Pull out the piston rod as far as possible and install the bottom cover and spring. Be sure not to forget the installation of the spring guide. After this, install the cover and compress the spring. Screw in the upper lock nut and install the upper metal. After finishing the assembling, check whether spring touches the cover or not by pressing down with hands.

2-5 DRIVE CHAIN

A Drive Chain Case

Chain case can be disassembled by removing four 6mm bolts. After disassembly clean the case and perform the necessary work.

B Drive Chain.

Chain is DK420, 98 links. Usually the chain can be taken off by removing engine left crankcase cover and removing joint clip. If you find difficulties, remove the under-half of the drive chain case, the chain will then be removed easily. If the chain adjuster becomes 'full out', cut a link from the chain. Before you cut the chain the second time check the sprocket at that time and replace sprocket if necessary. When you assemble the chain be sure to place the open end of clip facing opposite of movement of chain.

C Final Drive Flange

(1) Disassemble.

Remove the chain case, the chain and the rear wheel. Drive flange can be removed by releasing the sleeve nut and withdrawing axle sleeve. Take out the oil seal, bearings, and collars from the drive flange and wash them clean with a cleansing oil. Driven sprocket can be removed by releasing setting bolts.

(2) Inspection & Assemble.
(a) Wash the 6003Z ball bearing throughly. While holding it in hand and turn the outer race. If it doesn't turn, doesn't turn smoothly, or has excessive radius play, replace it.
(b) Replace the 23.357 oil seal if it is excessively torn, worn or distorted.
(c) Check the wear of the sprocket and the teeth where chain touches and replace sprocket if excessively worn. During assembling be sure to grease the bearing.
(d) Replace the damper rubber in the wheel hub if it is damaged or distorted.

Grease the bearing and install in the flange hub by use of a guide to the oil seal. Install the sprocket on the flange by the setting bolts firmly. Then lock them with the tongued washers. After setting the flange install the sleeve and be sure to put the collar on before installing rear fork. Install the flange loosely in order to adjust the chain.

2-6 FRONT AND REAR WHEEL

Standard tires are 2.25-17-4 ply. Rims made of steel. Spokes are #12 in size and 36 straight spokes for front; #10, #11 in size and 36 (half of each) for rear. Spokes are tightened by nipples on the end of the rim side. All nipples are tightened in turn. Be sure to tighten nipples with nipple spanner, feeling the tension by hand.

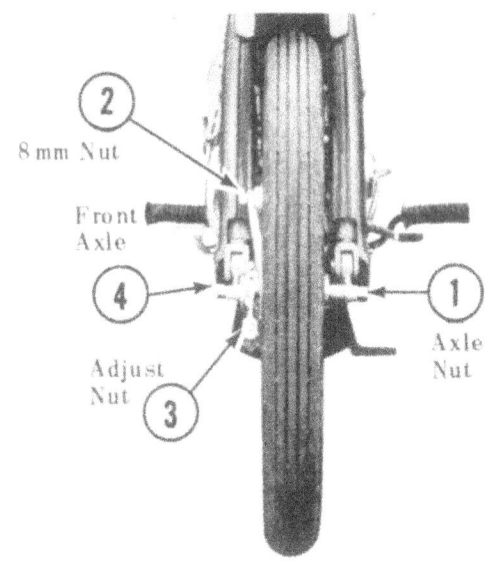

Fig. 26

A Front Wheel.
(1) Disassemble.
Put some support under the engine in order to float the front wheel and remove the nuts according to the directions shown on Fig. 26 1, 2, 3, and withdraw the (4) axle last, the front wheel will come out with the front brake. Usually 0202Z bearing can be taken out by hand, but if it is hard hammer the distance collar.

(2) Inspection and Assemble
(a) Check the trueness of the wheel and tire. Place the rim in a wheel testing stand for measuring the run-out and if it is bent or warped, replace it. Be sure to check the hub at the same time.
(b) Check the spokes and tighten them if needed.
(c) Check the wear of tires as well as for cuts, bruises or nails.
(d) Remove the 6202Z bearing in the hub and clean it. Check the smoothness of running and horizontal free play. If the play is excessive it should be replaced.
(e) Replace a bent or damaged axle.
(f) Speedometer gear must be easily turned. Grease if it doesn't run well. Also, check the speedometer pinion. When installing the wheel, ball bearings must be greased and assemble them with opposite procedure of disassembling. As a matter of fact, install the speedometer gear on to the wheel hub before assembling the wheel to the fork. Tightening of torque of axle is shown below.

3.5 - 4.5 Kg-m (25 - 35 ft.-lb.)

Fig. 27

B Rear Wheel

(1) Disassembling Rear Wheel

After putting the stand down remove the rear brake adjustment nut and torque arm anchor nut. See fig. 27. After removing the rear axle nut (left side) pull out the rear axle (3) with chain adjuster (4). Remove the side collar and pull the wheel to the right side in order to detach the drive flange and take out the wheel from frame by tilting the vehicle. After removing the rear wheel from frame, take out the 6301 bearing and oil seal. Usually bearings can be taken out by hand, but if it is too tight, hammer it lightly from inside using a soft drift.

(2) Inspection & Assembly.

(a) The rear wheel has to be checked by the same procedure as the front wheel check and necessary repairs made according to specifications.

(b) Spokes also must be checked by the same procedure of front wheel. Tighten if loose.

(c) Check the tires as on front.

(d) Check the rubber "O" ring (40.5 mm) which is on drum boss and replace it when it is damaged or collapsed.

(e) Wash 6301 bearing thoroughly and check the free play and roughness. Replace it if it is in bad condition.

(f) Check the lip of the oil seal and replace if distorted or damaged. Install the bearing with grease and install the "O" ring to the boss following the procedure exactly opposite of disassemble. After tightening the brake torque bolt, be sure to put the cottor pin in place. When replacing the axle, do not forget the mark on the drive chain adjuster. The mark goes up -- There is a left and right -- Tightening torque is 4.0-4.5 Kgm (25 - 35 ft.-lb.).

After tightening the axle nut, tighten the adjuster nut of the chain puller.

NOTES: (1) Check the drive chain after finishing assembling for tension (should be about 1" up and down movement when it is on the stand. If chain is old or used check it at its tightest spot).

(2) Be careful not to forget to install the "O" ring and not to damage it.

C Tire, Tube.

Tires—Air Pressure

The tires are more easily to be worn out than other parts, and tire pressures have much effect on steering and comfortable riding. Check the tires and air pressure before riding.

The pressures should not be higher nor lower than those recommended. The recommended pressures for the C110 are:

	solo	pillion carrier occupied
Front	22 lbs. p.s.i.	28 lbs. p.s.i.
Rear	28 lbs. p.s.i.	38 lbs. p.s.i.

Check the tire pressure especially when riding with a pillion passenger or heavy luggage.

Check the valve for leakage. See that the valve cap is fitted properly.

After a ride, wash off oil and scrape mud off the tires, and inspect the tire to see if they have picked up any nails, any pieces of glass or any pebbles, and if any, take it off. If a tire leaks, get it repaired without delay.

The tire bead is closely pressed to the rim to be air-tight only by the air pressure within the tube. With a pressure too low, air-tightness is imperfect, and therefore, the tube would creep around the rim and pull the tire valve out of itself and the tire wall will fracture.

On the contrary, with a pressure too high, the tire tread in contact with the ground is narrower, and the tread only is more rapidly worn, and the tires do not absorb road shocks as well.

(1) Repairing Tube
Removing tire —
Unscrew valve cap, remove valve plunger with key on valve cap. Unscrew valve nut.
Lay the wheel on a surface which should be level.
Press the tire down all the way round until it is completely clear of the rim.
Starting at the valve, lever the wall of the tire over the rim. Work around the tire with the second tire lever, leaving the first lever holding the starting point. When one side of the tire is taken off the tube can easily be taken out.
Tire levers are in the tool kit.

(2) Repairing tire tube—
Find the hole made in the tube. Then file around the hole with file and coat some rubber cement on the tube and a patching piece of rubber. After leaving them for a few minutes, stick to each other.

(3) Refitting the tire—
Insert the tube valve through the hole in the rim and screw down the nut. Set the tube around the rim taking care that it is not twisted. When refitting the tire, start opposite of the valve.

2-7 BRAKE

A Front Brake

(1) Disassemble
Follow the procedure for removing the front wheel. If you can remove one shoe with springs on by pulling over cam, you can also take out the other shoe. After removing the shoe, take off the brake arm and then the cam.

(2) Inspection & Assembly
(a) Measure the diameter of panel spacer and replace it if it is unserviceable.
(b) Measure the inner diameter of panel sleeve and replace the panel if over correction limit.
(c) If the diameter of brake cam is worn excessively, replace it. Also replace it if it is worn excessively at the cam part.
(d) If the shoe springs are collapsed, replace them.
(e) If the thickness of brake shoes are worn excessively replace them with shoe assemblies.
(f) Replace the oil seal if the lip is distorted or damaged.
(g) Replace the felt ring if it is in bad condition.
Assembly can be done following the procedure opposite of disassemble. File the brake shoes if there is any obstacles. Speedometer gear box is molded into the panel, so be sure to install the speedometer gear into the receiver before installing gear into the panel. Also check the wheel hub drum and perform any repairs needed.

B Rear Brake

Disassembling and assembling can be completed by exactly the same procedure of the front brake. (One exception is there isn't a spacer on the rear brake.)

2-8   FUEL TANK AND SADDLE

   A   Disassembling

   Loosen the rear cushion upper bolt and pull the seat backward and the seat will be detached.
   Fuel tank is held on with the bolt which can be seen after removing the seat. After removing fuel hoses, pull gas tank backwards. The fuel cock can be removed from assembly by removing the cup packing, filter and 6 mm screws.

   B   Inspection and Assembly
   (1) Replace the fuel tank front and rear rubber cushions if they are damaged or distorted.
   (2) Replace or repair the tank if there is leaks.
   (3) Replace the tank filter cap packing if it is damaged or distorted. Check the vent holes in the gas cap. Make sure the holes are open.
   (4) Replace the clip if it is collapsed. Also replace the fuel feed tube if the end part is damaged. Be sure to check the attaching part at assembly.
   (5) Check the cushion rubber and springs of saddle (double seat).

2-9   AIR CLEANER

   A   Disassemble

   Remove the air cleaner cover then remove the 6 mm screw. The air cleaner element can then be removed from the frame.

   B   Inspection and Assembly
   (1) Air cleaner must be checked regularly and replace the element whenever damaged or dirty.
   If the element gets wet be sure to wait until it dries before installing.
   (2) If the air cleaner is damaged or frayed replace the air cleaner element.
   Assemble air cleaner element exactly opposite of disassembling.

NOTES: Please make sure there are no holes to leak between air cleaner and engine. Leaks make the air cleaner useless and will wear out the engine much faster. It also makes the carburetor hard to adjust.

2-10   EXHAUSTS

   A   Disassemble & Assemble

   Detach the exhaust pipe joint from engine and remove three 6 mm muffler attaching bolts. The muffler can be removed together with the exhaust pipe at the same time.
   Diffuser pipe can be withdrawn by unscrewing the 5 mm attaching bolt in rear. If this is done you must enrichen the fuel mixture— Do not fail to do this.
   Replace the muffler packing if it is damaged or distorted. Also replace the exhaust pipe gasket if it is damaged.

NOTES: Once in a while (about every 2500 miles) it is good to remove the diffuser pipe and clean the carbon out of the holes. If holes become plugged up it will create back pressure and could harm the engine.

2-11   STEP BAR, MAIN STAND & BRAKE PEDAL

   A   Disassemble, Inspection

   Step bar can be removed by unscrewing the four 8 mm nuts which hold the step bar to the crankcase stud bolts. The main stand and brake pedal can be removed by following procedure. First, unscrew the brake adjust nut and remove the brake rod from rear brake arm, then remove the brake pedal return spring and main stand spring and withdrawing the rear brake pivot pipe, brake pedal and main stand will be removed.

(1) If there is a big clearance between brake pivot pipe and brake pedal, replace it, according to the specification.
(2) Replace brake pedal spring, main stand spring and brake rod spring if rusted or collapsed excessively.
(3) If the main stand is bent, either replace or repair. Wash all parts thoroughly before assembling and grease the main stand pipe and the inner part of the brake pedal pipe.

2-12 FRAME

A Disassemble, Inspection

Doing all the ways of removing the parts from frame, the frame will become the shape shown on Fig. 28.

(1) Check the detached part of weldings. Either replace or repair if any part is cracked, distorted or damaged on the pipe or pressed section of frame.
(2) Check for warpage, distortion and out-of-center. Check the angle of head pipe also. These are obvious faults, replace the frame.
(3) Replace the 3/16" steel balls if they are scratched or unevenly worn.
(4) Replace the top and bottom ball race when it is damaged, worn or scratched.

Tightness between ball race and head pipe is 1/100 - 5/100mm so they can be removed by tapping it from inside. At installing, be sure to install by using wooden hammer or a board in order not to be installed cocked to one side.

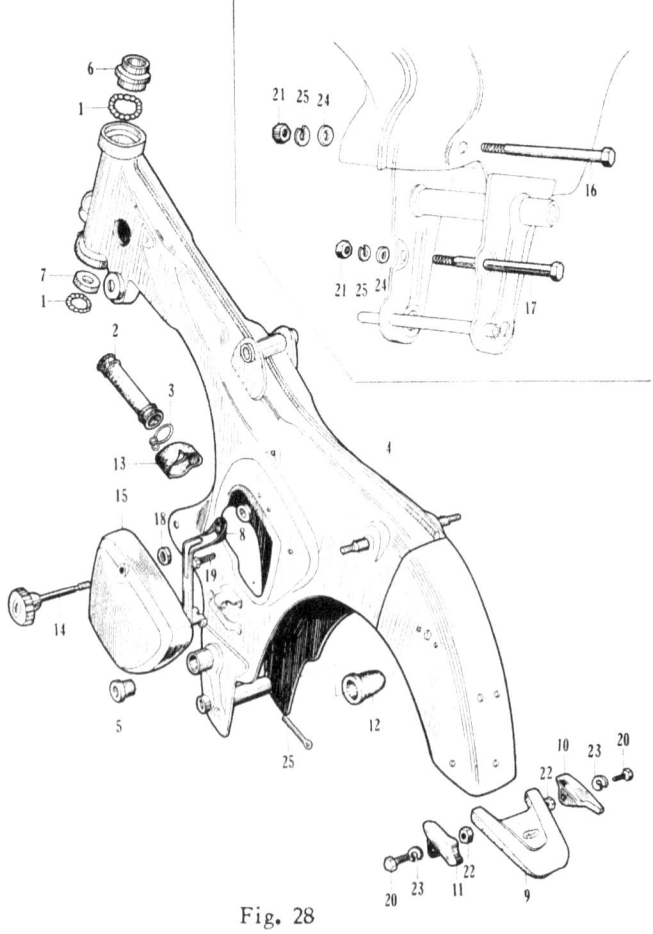

#	Part	Qty
1	Steel Ball	42
2	Manifold Rubber Tube	1
3	Manifold Rubber Tube Clip	2
4	Frame	1
5	Bushing Rear Pivot Bulb	2
6	Steering Top Ball Race	2
7	Steering Bottom Ball Race	1
8	Battery Stay	1
9	Rear Fender Mud Guard	1
10	R. Rear Fender Mud Guard Stay	1
11	L. Rear Fender Mud Guard Stay	1
12	Muffler Setting Bar Cap	1
13	Carburetor Joint Cover	1
14	Latch, Tool Box	1
15	Battery Box	1
16	Support Bolt A	1
17	Rear Engine Bolt	1
18	Tool Box Latch Stop Nut	1
19	Bolt	1
20	Screw	2
21	Hex Nut	2
22	Hex Nut	2
23	Lock Washer	2
24	Washer	2
25	Lock Washer	2

Fig. 28

MEMO

III. ELECTRICAL SYSTEM

3-1 IGNITION SYSTEM

The series of system from magneto, contact braker, condenser, spark plug and others is called the electrical system. The high tension electrical current, generated by the high tension coil of magneto, is transmitted to spark plug at specific intervals by the operation of contact breaker and ignites fuel mixture.

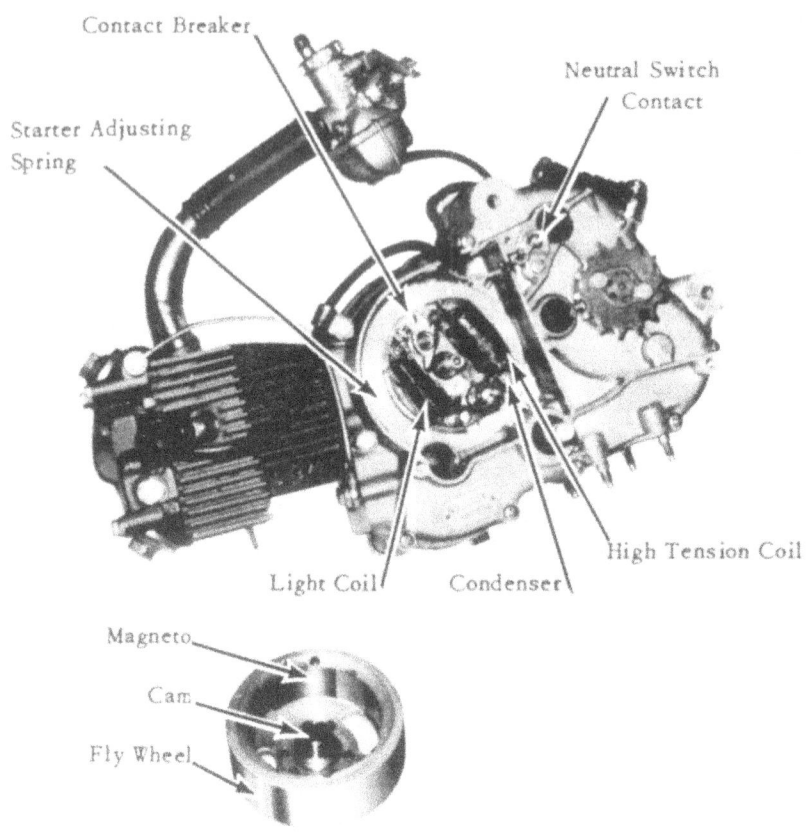

Fig. 29

A. Contact Breaker

As illustrated in fig. 29, the contact breaker is installed onto the stator of the magneto. Point cam is machined to boss part of flywheel and is adjusted from flywheel hole.

(1) Disassembling

Remove flywheel in manner described in engine chapter.
Next remove wire terminal of contact breaker primary circuit, loosen screw securing breaker and take off breaker.

(2) Inspection & Maintenance

Contact area of point should have bright metal finish and be smooth. If discolored black or brownish or facing rough and uneven, file down both faces at same time with a point file, if the defects are minor. If defects are major, disassemble and grind off rough or uneven face separately with oil stone. Replace the assembly if it can't be corrected. After furbishing, wash off points with gasoline and wipe clean, before reassembling. Be careful not to leave any oily film on facings as it will cause scoring and wear again.

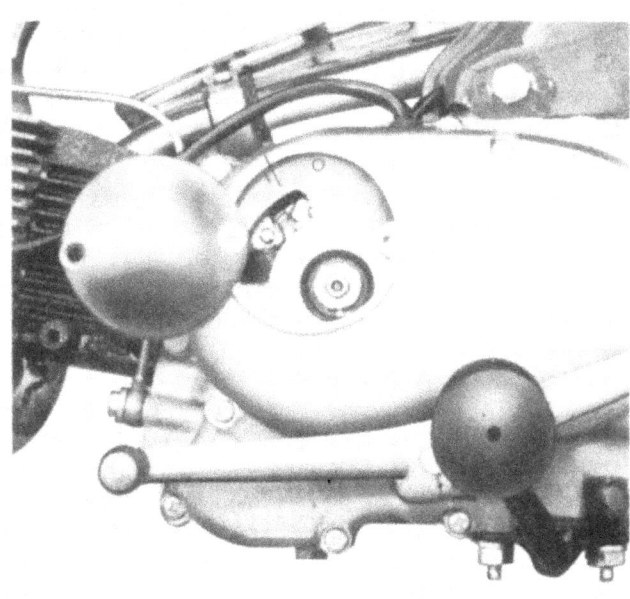

Fig. 30

(3) Reassembling & Adjustments

Fit point axis to base hole and secure with screw. If oil is not penetrating oil felt at this time, penetrate with engine oil. Adjust after securing flywheel. Make sure key groove is fitted securely with woodruff key before tightening flywheel to standard torque 20 ft-lb (2.8 kg-m). After installing left cover adjust ignition timing to 35° B.T.C.D. Use timing marks.

Adjustment is done by loosening screw (a), inserting driver into slit (b) and turning. After adjusting, rotate flywheel about 90° and check to see that gap between points is within limit of 0.3 - 0.4 mm (0.012 - 0.016").

B. Condenser

Condenser is installed onto magneto as in fig. 29. Construction and wiring is as in fig. 31. The condenser prevents arcing at the points and aids in breaking down the magnetic field in the coil, helping the operation of the contract breaker.
Capacity is 0.2 - 0.26 μf.

To determine condition of condenser measure insulation of condenser primary coil side terminal and shell with service tester, with point in opened position.

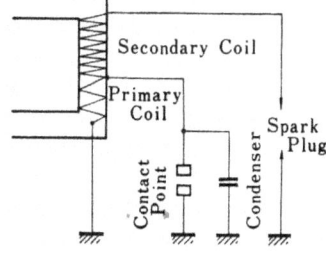

Fig. 31 Wiring Diagram of Ignition System

Under normal temperature, if insulation resistance measures;

    over 5 meg. ohm   good
    1 - 5 meg. ohm   fair
    under 1 meg. ohm   no good

and determine according to the above findings. To replace, remove screw and connector and take off.

Condenser itself rarely causes trouble, only be careful of securely tighten and that point of

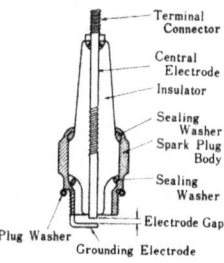

Fig. 32 Section View of Spark Plug

contact is clean as these can be because of faulty ignition.

C. Spark Plug

Standard type is N.G.K. make, C-7HW type and fig. 32 illustrates sectional diagram.

Use plug wrench to remove, paying caution not to damage insulator. Plug should be wholly dry and have a thin accumulation of grey or brownish coating and the insulator scorched golden brown color.

Clean if found dirty and if carbon has deposited. After cleaning, set electrode gap to 0.6 - 0.7 mm. Replace if spark plug is in bad condition.

Condition of Spark Plug	Engine Condition	Probable Cause	Probable Remedy
Inside of plug dirty, sooty or wet, etc.	Hard starting, engine misfires at low speed.	Plug too cold.	Change to hot plug **C7HW** (Consult technician).
		Carburetor mixture too rich. Excessive use of choke.	Correctly adjust carburetor.
		Driving abnormally long at low speed.	Avoid as much as possible. Change to hot type plug **C7HW** if necessary.
		Burning oil due to worn piston rings.	If excessive, disassemble and repair engine.
		Damaged top insulator. Usage of deteriorated high tension wiring.	Replace plug.
		Contact point dirty.	Clean points.
		Firing gap too large.	Adjust gap.
Insulator is white without hardly any accumulation of foreign matter.	Poor operation at high speed and hill climbing.	Plug too hot causing preignition	Change to cold type plug. (Consult technician).
		Gas leakage due to faulty installation of plug.	Replace with new gasket. Tighten to correct torque.
		Carburetor mixture too lean.	Correct to right adjustment.
		Faulty ignition timing.	Correct to right adjustment.
Igniting part of insulator damaged.		Using too hot a plug.	Change to cold type plug.
		Overheat due to plug loosely tightened.	Tighten to correct torque.

Fig. 34

To install, first tighten the plugs "finger tight" then turn 1/4 with plug wrench. Do not forget to place plug washer.

Check condition of plug with plug tester after cleaning and setting. Usually bad condition of plug cannot be determined visually except for worn electrode or other visible damage.

D. Flywheel Magneto

For domestic two types, FA Type (Kokusan Denki) and HDM Type (Nippon Denso) of same performance are used, and for overseas, only HDM Type is used. This is installed on left side of engine. A permanent magnet, cast into flywheel, rotates around iron core coil. There are two coils installed on the base. One a light coil, the other an ignition coil.

(1) Testing the Ignition Coil.

Take off plug cap of coil secondary wiring end and connect lead line of three needles tester (On service tester). At the time of kick, measure the maximum gap that spark can constantly jump with the needles. If this gap is under 6 mm the coil is faulty or the magnet is weak and necessary action must be taken. Usually it is attributed to faulty coil. If charging performance of light coil is deteriorating probable cause could demagnetization.

(2) Disassembly, replacement & reassembly of ignition coil

Remove flywheel, take off stator assembly and pull off cord from case and unscrew ignition coil. Install ignition coil so that iron core face fits with grooved facing of stator base, in correct position. After passing cord through case, insert grommet properly and tighten on stator base.

(3) Demagnetization of flywheel magnet.

When magnet force demagnetizes have this re-magnetized at shop that specializes in this kind of work. Usually, natural loss of magnet force does not occur so it is necessary to check lead line of coil for shorts with tester.

3.2 CHARGING SYSTEM

Charging system consists of low tension coil of magneto, selenium rectifier, battery and associated wiring.

Alternating current generated by magneto goes to head lamp, tail lamp and meter lamp and a part of this flow to charge battery. Alternating current is rectified to half wave current by selenium rectifier before going to battery.

A. Charging Coil

Low tension coil is separated into coil for lamps and for charging. For night driving this generates alternate current (6 - 8V) direct to the head lamp, tail lamp and meter lamp to light these and the charging coil generates alternate current day and night to charge battery.

(1) Testing the charge coil.

In order to determine condition of charge coil, connect ammeter (reading about 2 A) in series to fuse connector, start the engine and check current according to the crank revolutions.

Check with key in daytime and night-time positions. Standard charging capacity for each position at different revolutions is according to following list. If charge is more or less 20 - 30% than as indicated replace coil.

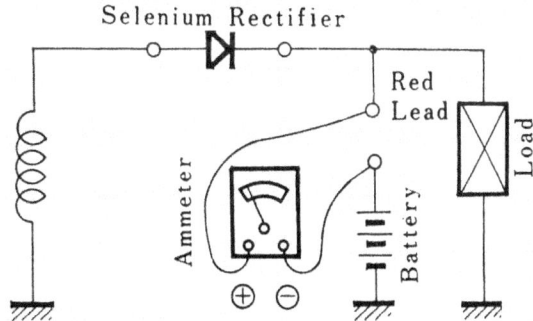

Wiring Ammeter for Checking Coil Charge

Crank rpm		1,500	3,000	6,000	8,000
Daytime Charging Current (A)		0	0.2	0.2	1.5
Night-time	Charging Current (A)	0	0.2	0.4	0.5
	Lamp Voltage (V)	4.5	6.5	8.0	8.5

Fig. 33

(2) Replacement

Be careful to center iron core with stator base, as with high tension coil, when installing.

B. Selenium Rectifier

Selenium rectifier is installed on inside of frame. (Fig. 36) This charges the battery by rectifying half wave the alternate current generated by the coil.

By removing the battery at daytime or running long distance at high speed without a fuse will cause reverse flow current towards selenium rectifier causing it to lose it's rectifying efficiency and if this is continued for a prolonged period the rectifier will get hot and may break. Be sure to check that fuse is not blown out and is properly installed.

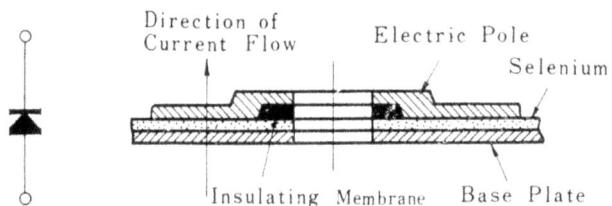

Sectional View of Slenium Rectifier

Fig. 35

If battery discharges too often, check not only the coil, but also discoloring of rectifier and for short of terminals. After replacing parts, securely tighten terminals.

C. Battery (See fig. 36)

Horn, directional signal lamp, neutral lamp and others are run by the direct current flowing from the battery. The battery used is MBCI-6 type, which has three cells, whose plates are connected in series. Capacity is 6V-2Ah, and has discharge capacity of 10 hours at 0.2A. This is connected from selenium rectifier through fuse (red lead line), and black terminal is grounded to frame through main switch.

Battery is located on left side of frame and can be easily inspected by removing battery cover.

(1) Removal & installation of battery

Remove battery band, disconnect fuse connector and take battery out. Check to see fuse is in place and for short of fuse when installing battery. Always keep outside of battery washed clean so inside can be seen. Ground part should be checked for rust and corrosion and securely tightened.

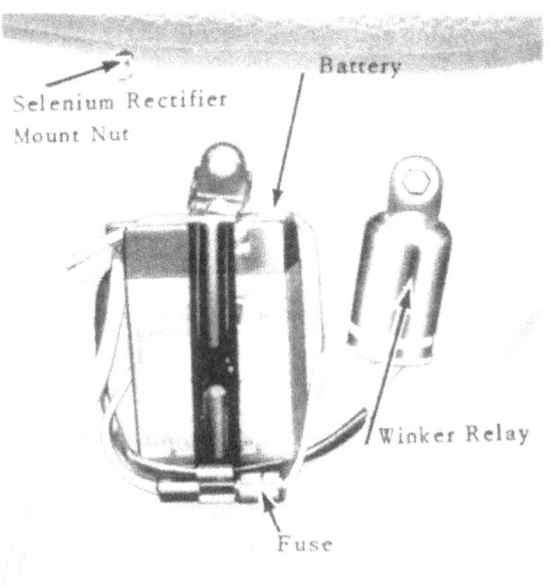

Fig. 36

(2) Inspection & maintenance.

This should be periodically checked by the user or dealer.
Just checking of electrolyte level is sufficient, but dealer should also check its specific gravity.

Specific gravity will determine batteries charging rate performance as follows.

Specific gravity	Rate of charging
1.130 - 1.500	0% (full charg)
1.200 - 1.210	50% (half ″)
1.260	100% (none ″)

The above are for standard figures at $20°$ C and for approximate calculations at different temperatures use the following formula.

$$\text{Specific gravity at } 20°C - (t°C \text{ spec. grav.}) - 0.0007(t° - 20°)$$

40- 50% discharge necessitates charging.

If battery discharge continues, sulphation (white powder form on plates) will form on plates and settle in bottom of cell. In this case wash out cell completely and refill with battery electrolyte before charging. This is done at a battery shop.

MEMO

3.3 SWITCHES

A. Combination Switch

A combination switch is separated into three positions:

(Position of Key) (Operation)

0 - Key can be removed when stopped or parked.
Black wiring from contact breaker terminal is ground inside switch and engine will not start. Terminal wiring from battery is disconnected inside switch and all electrical apparatus will not function.

1 - Daytime driving and key cannot be removed.
Black wiring from contact breaker terminal is released from ground and engine will start. Battery terminal wiring is grounded and horn, directional signal lamp and neutral lamps will operate by turning attached switch.

2 - Night-time driving and key cannot be removed.
Head lamp, meter lamp and tail lamps will light besides the functions of position 1. However as lighting is from magneto these will not light unless engine is running.

NO.	DESCRIPTION
	Combination Horn & Dimmer Switch
1	Upper Horn Button Switch Case
2	Lower Horn Button Switch Case
3	Horn Button Switch Terminal Ass'y
4	Horn Button Switch Conduct Holder
5	Spring Horn Button Switch Contact
6	Slide Ball Horn Button Switch
7	Knob Horn Button Switch
8	Contact Horn Button Switch
9	Spring Horn Button Holder
10	Push Button Horn Switch
11	Clamp
12	Spring Horn Button
	Starter Switch Ass'y
13	Case Upper Winker Switch
14	Case Lower Winker Switch
15	Terminal Ass'y Winker Switch
16	Holder Winker Switch Contact
17	Knob Winker Switch
18	Contact Winker Switch
19	Clamp
20	Adjuster Throttle Grip
21	Screw
22	Screw
23	Screw

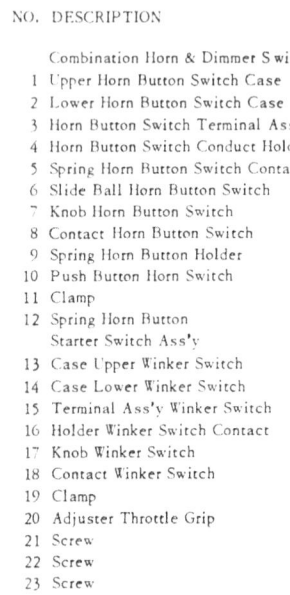
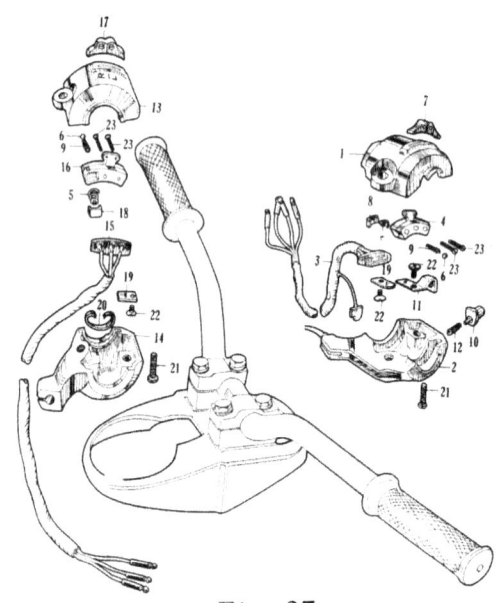

Fig. 37

If the above three positions do not operate properly when turning switches on, first check wiring system of the defective part. If it still does not function conclude that the combination switch is defective and replace. In order to check defect of switch itself, make a conduct test.

B. Directional Signal Lamp Switch & Head Dimmer Switch

Directional signal lamp switch is on right side of handle and head light dimmer switch is on left side of handle. These both have the same kind of construction. If control knob does not operate, or contact points are defective or if wiring system has short, these can be disassembled and repaired. Replace parts, if necessary.

Disassembly & Inspection (See fig. 37)

Loosen screw holding together grip metal and disassemble into top and bottom piece. Remove metal fastener of switch terminal. If terminal or ball facing is corroded, rusted, shorted, etc., take fine emery paper and polish for better contact. If further replacement is required take off handle mounting nut, so handle can be lifted up, take off head lamp and remove concealed connector. Pull out harness on side that requires replacing. Reassembly is the opposite of this, but be careful in passing harness through and not pinch lead lines when tightening.

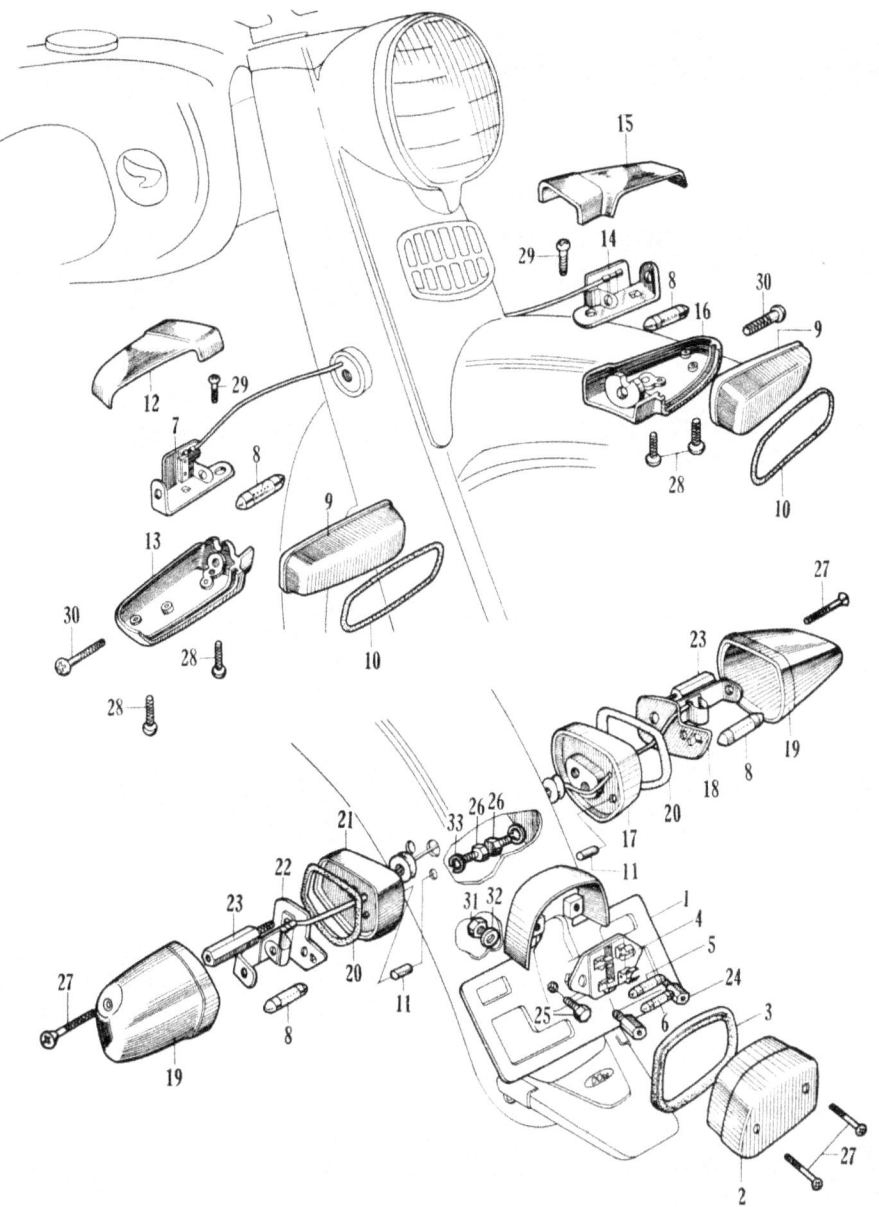

WINKER TAIL LAMP

Fig. 38

1. Number Plate Bracket
2. Tail Lite Ass'y
2. Tail Lite Lens
3. Tail Lite Lens Packing
4. Tail Lite Socket Ass'y
5. Stop Lite Bulb
6. Tail Lite Bulb
7. R. Front Winker Socket
8. Winker Bulb
9. Front Winker Lens
10. Front Winker Lens Packing
11. Front Winker Base Knock Pin
12. R. Front Winker Upper Case
13. R. Front Winker Under Case
14. L. Front Winker Socket Comp
15. L. Front Winker Upper Case
16. L. Front Winker Under Case
17. R. Rear Winker Base
18. R. Rear Winker Socket Comp
19. Rear Winker Lens
20. Rear Winker Lens Packing
21. L. Rear Winker Base
22. L. Rear Winker Socket Comp.
23. Front Winker Socket Setting Bolt
24. Tail Lite Ass'y Setting Bolt
25. Bolt
26. Bolt
27. Screw
28. Screw
29. Screw
30. Screw
31. Hex Nut
32. Flat Washer
33. Lock Washer

C. Neutral Switch (See fig. 39)

Neutral switch is located on right side of crankcase and operates together with gear shift mechanism.

Poor functioning of neutral lamp can be sometimes attributed to the switch itself. The causes are poor contact of switch contact and switch rotor, short due to damage of resin mold part of contact, wiring cut or shorted, etc. When replacing switch also check to see if rubber ring is in good condition or not, before installing.

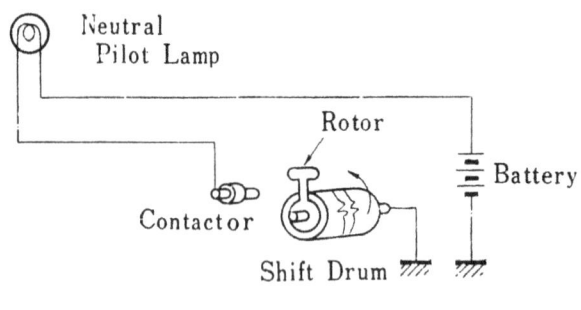

Fig. 39

D. Horn Button Switch

This is installed on the grip metal of left side handle. As this is a simple push button, if horn does not blow it is usually caused by poor contact of button. This can be repaired by using a fine emery paper. As the harness for this part is combined with head light dimmer switch, replacement is done together.

3.4 VARIOUS ELECTRICAL LOADS, HARNESS & SPEEDOMETER

A. Horn

This is of direct current microphonic type and construction. Tone volume is 90 - 100 phone at 2 m distant and requires current of 0.6 - 0.8A at this time.

When volume of sound is poor or tone is hoarse the cause is usually not the horn itself, but discharge of battery, poor contact of horn button switch, etc., so first check to see if anything is wrong with these before checking horn itself.

To disassemble, remove head lamp, take off bolt (6 mm) holding head lamp case. Horn is installed behind head lamp case so remove this and connect horn to 6 V battery and check. Tone and volume is adjusted by turning in or out the adjusting screw. If this cannot be repaired, replace with new one.

Upon reassembling check all attaching places for rust and make for good ground then install securely.

B. Directional Signal Lamp Relay (See fig. 40)

This is installed on the right side of body and is of relay type as illustrated in fig. 39. This blinks by the balance of the relay pulling power and electrical current. Standard operation is 70 - 110 blinks per minute.

With key in "on" position, if one lamp on same side is out the other lamp will not blink. In this case replace the burned out lamp.

When operating the switch, if one side functions correctly and the other side does not, or both sides function

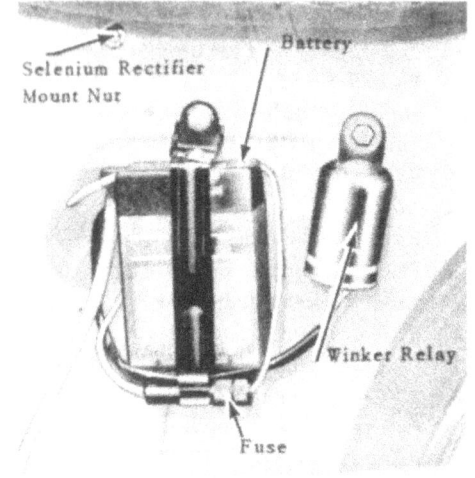

Fig. 40

at the same time this trouble is not in the relay, but always in the directional signal lamp switch, wiring, lamp, etc.

With directional signal lamp switch on, if either side does not blink and stays on all the time, or the blinking is erratic, or it does not light at all the trouble is in the relay. In this case replace the relay. Also, in the event it does not light at all the trouble may be lead wiring broken from the battery to the relay or bad connection.

C. Speedometer

This is of magnetic eddy type and incorporates two devices—the speedometer to indicate rate of car speed and odometer to record the distance traveled.

Speedometer reads 60 mph when meter cable rotates at 1,400 rpm and odometer registers 1 km when meter cable rotates 1,400 rpm.

When speedometer glass breaks, inside of glass mists, indicator needle comes off or does not register correctly, replace speedometer itself. Follow speedometer clamp and it will off from handle.

Inner cable and speedometer axle should be correctly fitted and tightened.

D. Head Lamp

As lens and reflector of head lamp (fig. 41) are sealed together into one piece, bulb is replaced from behind reflector. Therefore, it is not necessary to touch inside of the reflector, which prevents misting of the lens and reflector. This construction also prevents dust from getting inside.

Bulbs of 6 - 8 V, 10W (12 W when dimmed) are specified. If specified parts are not used, not only will the set brightness not be achieved, but will burn out when revolution is increased.

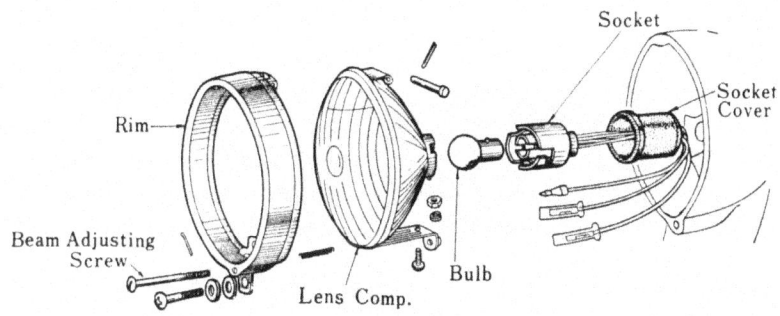

Fig. 41

To replace, remove head lamp, pull off socket cover and twist socket body and take out socket assembly. Remove bulb from socket.

When either head lamp burns out, do not run without lights, but switch over to the good lamp and ride until replacement can be made. Be careful not to run over 1 - 2 minutes with lamp burned out as the tail lamp and speedometer lamp will become overloaded and burn out. Head lamp beam aiming is done by screwing in beam adjusting screw with driver.

E. Tail Lamp & Speedometer Lamp

With switch on in night position head, speedometer and tail lamps all operate together and only light when engine is running.

Tail lamp is of 6 - 8 V, 2 W, speedometer lamp is a special type 6 - 8V 1 W.

Only use specified tail lamp and speedometer lamp, otherwise it burn out or not light sufficiently.

For replacing, gauge lamp is done so by removing head light and tail lamp by taking off tail lens.

F. Directional Signal Lamp

With engine switch on, right side front and rear directional signal lamp will function when pushing control knob forward. Pulling knob towards back will light left side.

Lamps used (4 pieces) are all 6 - 8 V 8 W. These are replaced by removing screws of each lens.

G. Fuse - See page 26

As illustrated in fig. 36 fuse is installed on the battery + cord. Fuse is 7 A. The cause of the fuse blowing out is a short in the wiring system. Repair the troubled parts and replace fuse. Never use copper wire, fuse or larger amp. than specified or any other metal object because if electrical circut shorts current of about 20 amp. will flow through circuit and burn the switches and harness and may result in a fire of wire harness.

H. Wire Harness

Electrical of wiring system are put together with the exception of the connector sections, and are protected by vinyl tubing and passed through frame. As tail lamp and left and right rear directional signal lamp wirings

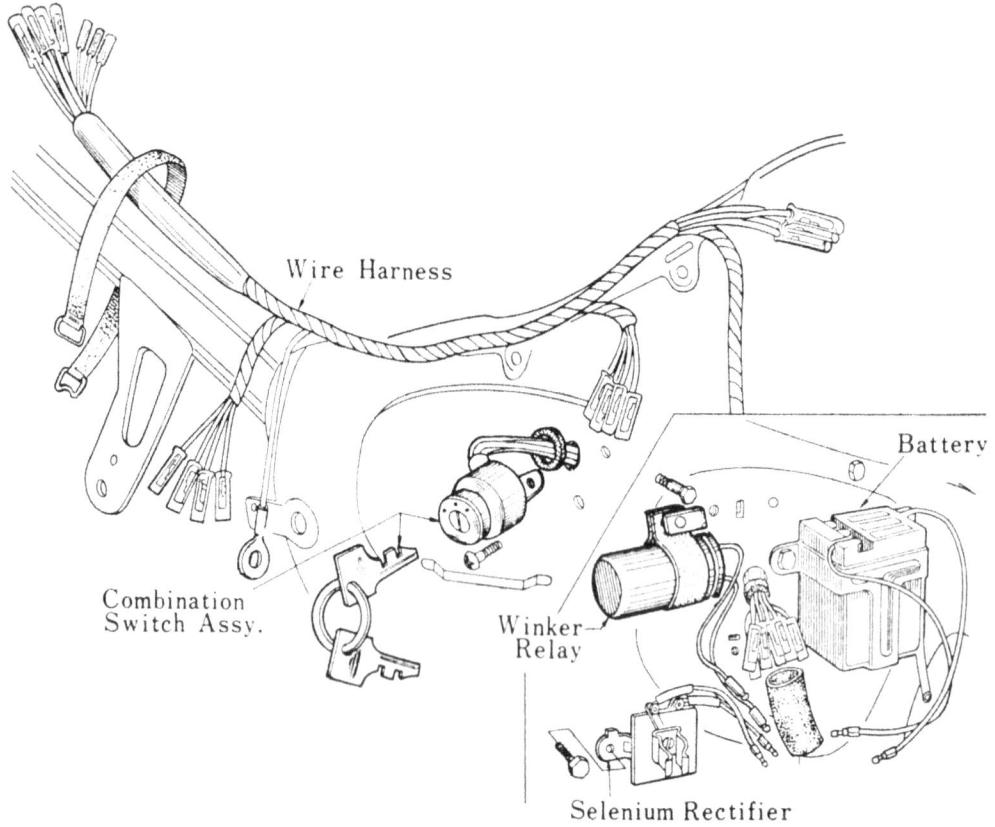

Fig. 42

passed through inside of welded part of rear fender, pull out each wire one by one so as not to force, when removing harness. When installing also do not force. There are clamps at various intervals, so set and securely fasten these clamps and grommets. Be sure to match connectors with wiring colors, when connecting.

MEMO

MEMO

IV. INSPECTION, MAINTENANCE & SPECIFICATION

4.1 PREVENTIVE MAINTENANCE

In the previous chapters maintenance and adjustments have been taken up for each system or parts. "Preventive Maintenance" is to carry out diagnosis, maintenance, adjustment, etc., of these various parts and systems at periodical intervals from a different stand point. At times, maintenance is carried out partly in order to maintain the performance of the vehicle.

A. Engine Tune-Up

Engine tune-up is a means to restore the engine performance back to normal and is a rectifying operation, not just as inspection. The performance of the engine is governed by the following conditions and by rectifying these, one by one, the engine can be restored to normal operation.

Compression System
Ignition System
Intake System
Combusion System
Fuel System

By fulfilling the requirements of these 5 basic operations, performance as an internal combustion engine will be complete. The following are the steps for checking and remedying the faults.

(1) Checking compression

If compression is low the engine will lose power and if for some reason there is compression loss the engine revolution will become uneven and will cause engine to stall at low idle.

To measure compression follow the following steps.

Operation Steps	Remarks
① Remove spark plugs.	Use plug wrench
② Insert compression gauge in spark plug hole and hold tightly in place.	Make sure compression gases do not leak.
③ Open throttle grip and choke wide open, continuously kicking down kick pedal strongly.	Do not forget this or else readings will differ completely.
④ Watch gauge while kicking and take reading of needle at highest point.	Do not discontinue kicking until reading is taken as gauge will keeping rising with each kick.
⑤ **Correct reading is 120 to 140 lbs.**	Check when engine is warm.
⑥ If reading is above the correct compression, carbon has accumulated in combustion chamber.	Remove cylinder head and clean carbon. (see p. 4)
⑦ If reading is below the above limits there is compression loss in valve, piston rings, head gasket, etc.	Inspect tappets, disassemble, inspect and overhall others.

(2) Tightening of cylinder head

When compression is low first check tappet clearance, then check to see if head is securely tightened or not.

Operation Steps	Remarks
1. Remove head cover.	
2. Tighten cylinder head bolts.	Use small torque wrench.
3. Specified torque is 0.8 kg cm (60 lb/in)	
4. When cylinder stud bolts are tightened as specified (3), trouble is inside. Remove head and disassemble and inspect cylinder. After disassembling head, always tighten head according to above torque.	Repair head, cylinder, piston

(3) Adjusting tappet clearance

Tappet clearance has a great deal to do with the operation of the valves. When compression is low the tappets still operate and are the cause for the valves not to close completely. When tappet clearance is too large the tappet noise becomes loud, causing excessive engine noise. This clearance is therefore related to the power of the engine, performance at slow idle and excessive noise and is an important function.

Adjustment is by the following steps.

Operation Steps	Remarks
① Remove tappet cover.	
② Remove contact breaker cover.	
③ Check tappet clearance with "T" mark on flywheel and mark on case lined up.	
④ Tappet clearance is correct when .004" thickness gauge (a) will clear and .006" will not.	
⑤ Standard clearance is .004"	Check when cold.
⑥ When clearance is not correct, loosen adjusting nut and adjust with adjusting screw. After tightening adjusting nut, recheck clearance.	Use tappet adjusting box wrench and tappet lock box wrench. Be careful as clearance will change after tightening adjusting nut.

Fig. 43

(4) Adjusting ignition timing

When the ignition timing is wrong, even if the engine has proper compression and the valves operate in order, the engine will not perform sufficiently. When the timing is too fast or too slow it will cause over-heating or back firing and have very diverse results. Also, this is always in contact operation and must be periodically checked.

The following are the adjustment steps.

Step of Work	Remarks
① Align mark on flywheel and punched mark on case.	Provide the point gap as 0.3~0.4mm (0.012~0.016")
② Check contact facing of point through flywheel window.	Move flywheel slightly and open points. Can be easily seen by using light.
③ If facing uneven or burnt, file with point file. If facing extensively uneven remove and correct with oil stone. Place file between points to work both facings at once.	Be sure not to install points with oil on facing.
④ Ideal ignition timing is to have point contacts open instantly when the "T" mark on flywheel passes mark on case. Use tester for adjusting as operation is difficult to follow by eye.	
⑤ Take out connector of wire harness contained inside frame on top of engine, take off black wire and connect to black wire of tester. Ground red tester wire to body and turn tester switch on (Use point or service tester).	If tester is not available use lamp to check conduct. Use 6V miniature lamp. Connect the lead to contact breaker arm Ground to engine or frame Lamp The moment contact points open, the light will off Battery
⑥ Revolve flywheel slowly in direction of revolution and adjust so that lamp goes out instantly when mark passes case marking.	Correct timing can be obtained by adjusting as in (6). In other words ignition timing is 35° BTDC (stationary)
⑦ Adjustment is done by loosening screw 'a' and turning 'b' with screw driver. Right turn of driver advances and left turn retards. Fig. 44	
⑧ When position is correct tighten 'a'. After tightening recheck to make sure.	Position may change by tightening. Be careful.

(5) Cleaning and adjustment of spark plugs

Spark plugs must be periodically cleaned and adjusted or else it will not spark and ignite in best condition if dirty, damaged or electrode worn. If plug electrode is sooty, wet or have carbon accumulation these must be removed or else high tension current will escape through these foreign agents. For removal of this, use sand blaster (plug cleaner) which makes cleaning of plugs very easy.

When sand blaster is not available, clean with wire brush, brush and wipe off with dry cloth. When carbon has accumulated, pick off with sharp instrument. At this, time do not use burner and others to dry off as this will have a bad effect.

After cleaning, set electrode gap. Set gap so that 0.6 mm (0.024") thickness gauge will easily pass through by lifting or lightly tapping portion ⓐ.

Determine whether plug is good or bad after setting gap to standard clearance by using plug tester. In other words, set at predetermined voltage and if spark is constant under various inside pressures of tester this is in good condition. Replace if found bad. (see p. 24).

Fig. 45

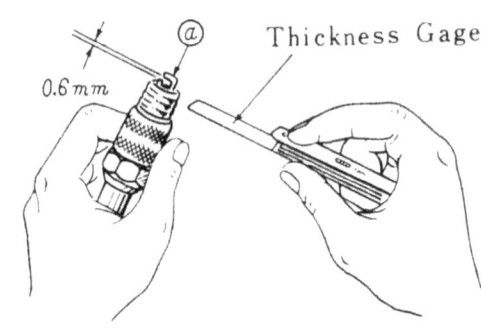
Fig. 46

(6) Ignition coil secondary sparking performance test

When there is trouble in the ignition coil, plug will not spark or will miss or will become weak and affect the firing.

In order to check this attach a good plug to secondary coil, kick engine over while grounding and confirm the plug sparking performance.

Also, there is a three needle spark coil tester. Connect + of tester to this + pole, ground - pole to body or engine and measure maximum gap that spark can jump, when kicking engine over. If this gap is over 6 mm (0.24"), coil is in good condition. However, check to be sure that trouble is not in coil as poor condenser can also be cause of trouble (see p. 24).

(7) Condenser test

Spark plug will not operate correctly when insulator inside condenser is poor and performance of condenser is defective and this is sometimes mistaken for bad ignition coil. Condition of condenser can be determined by measuring the insulator resistance of primary coil side and outside covering of condenser with service tester. (see p. 24).

(8) Fuel supplying system

When fuel system is stopped up engine will miss when accelerating or stop at high speed as fuel supply to carburetor is insufficient.

In this case check by the following steps.

Step for Work	Remarks
① If tank has sufficient fuel, check flowing condition by disconnecting fuel feed tube from carburetor elbow.	
② If flow is insufficient remove tank and clean out tank and inside of tube.	
③ Also reconnect fuel feed tube with carburetor and remove fuel cock. Check flow of gasoline when shutter is opened.	Check fuel cock by removing screw attaching to carburetor.
④ If cock is plugged up disassemble and clean.	

(9) Cleaning and adjustment of carburetor

Remove and clean carburetor every 8 months or 8,000 km. Other adjustments are to be performed as required. Steps for work and adjustment are as follows.

1. Set throttle stop screw (B) to engine rpm 800 - 1,000 rpm.

Adjust air fuel mixture by air screw (a). Proper position is when air screw is turned in fully, then turned back about 1 to 1-1/4 turns and when exhaust noise will not change even if body is tilted inside of 10° both ways.
Jet needle calibration alteration or adjustment of main jet, etc. is required if vehicle will not accelerate along with slow opening of grip when running vehicle or if maximum speeds cannot be obtained with grip fully opened.

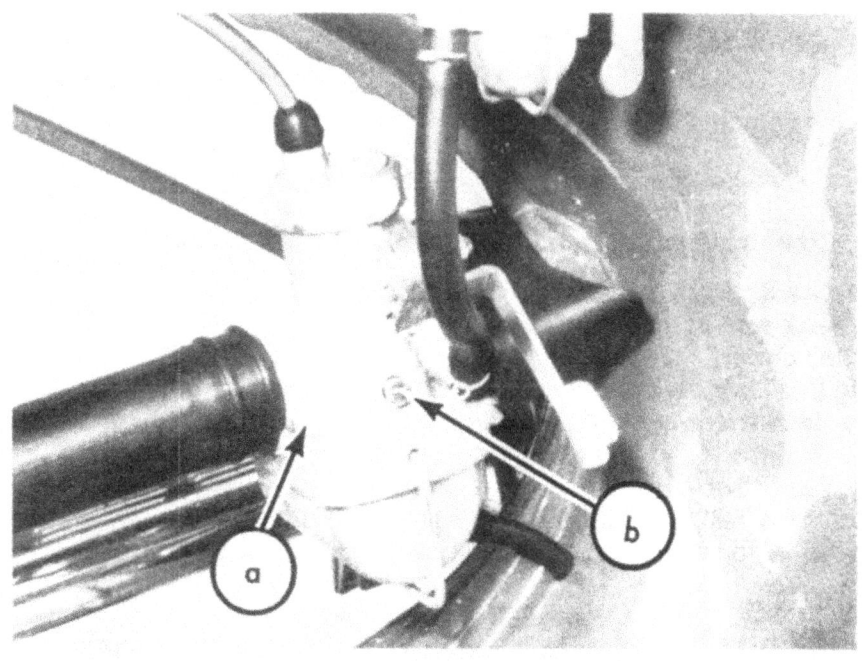

Fig. 47

Steps for Work
1. Remove 6mm nut holding carburetor.
2. Remove throttle wire, air cleaner connecting tube, fuel feed tube, etc.
3. Disassemble carburetor.
4. Wash disassembled parts with cleaning solvent.
5. Blow out each nozzle with compressed air, wash and clean, then adjust after reassembling and installing. Adjusting is usually done by idle adjustment.

(10) Cleaning of air cleaner

When air cleaner is clogged up with dust, intake air meets strong resistance and cannot be readily sucked in. Therefore, vehicle will lose power and when accelerating this cannot keep up with it. Periodically perform cleaning of air cleaner so the above events do not occur.

B. Adjustment of Drive Chain

Drive chain should always be tightened properly or it will create chain knock while running and hit against chain case if too slack. If chain tension is too strong this will create resistance and sufficient power will not be transmitted to rear wheels. Steps for adjusting are as follows.

Steps of Work	Remarks
① Remove peep hole cap of chain case	
② Loosen large and small nut securing rear wheel axle. Adjust rear wheel axle chain adjuster so that chain deflection is at its maximum 10~20mm, through chain case peep hole.	Set marking of adjuster and fork at same position on both sides.
③ Chain will tighten by tightening chain adjuster nut.	

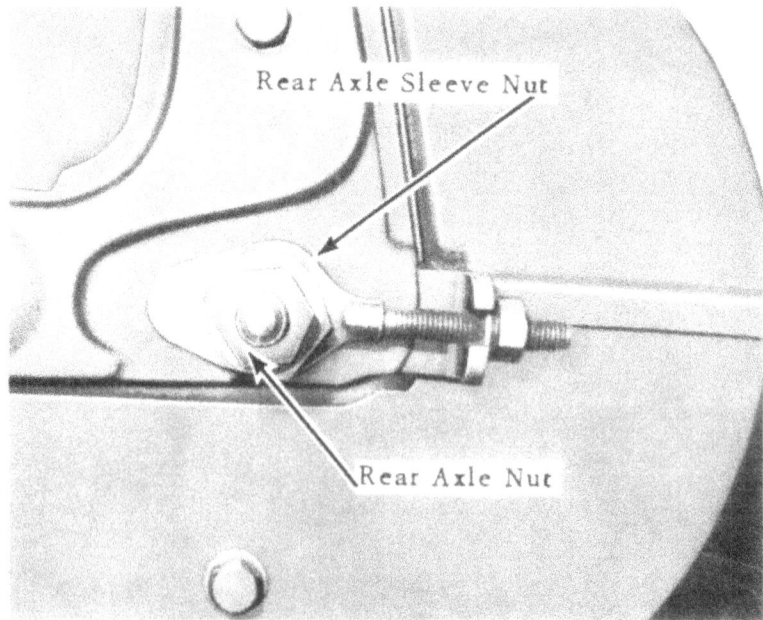

Fig. 48

C. Adjusting Brakes

As brakes are the staff of life these of course must be checked periodically and driver should also habitually check these before driving vehicle every day.

(1) Adjustment of front brakes

Adjust play of handle lever for front brake.

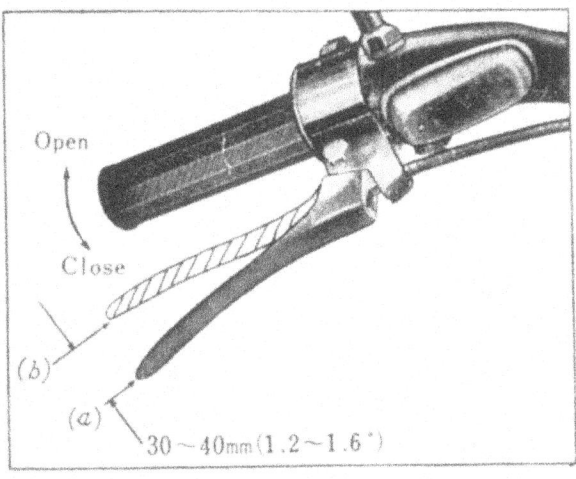
Fig. 49

Fig. 50

(2) Adjustment of rear brake free play.

Adjust free play of pedal for brake.

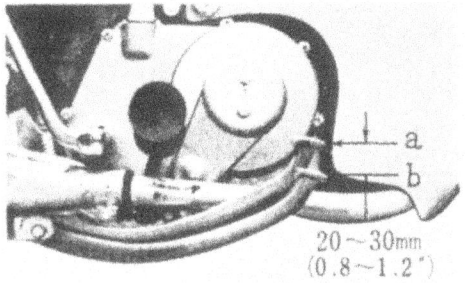

Steps for Adjusting	Remarks
① As same as front brake, free play will decrease by tightening nut (a) and increase by loosening.	
② Required free play is 20~30 mm (0.8~1.2″) from when pedal is in natural position till it starts to hold.	When adjusting allowance is gone, change angle of arm or replace brake shoe.

Fig. 51 Fig. 52

D. Care of Battery

Electrolyte of battery should be replenished at set intervals as this loses water after long usage.

When liquid level is lower than plates it shows that the battery capacity will decrease and discharge rapidly. Therefore liquid should always be filled to correct quantity. When liquid drops down to a minimum level, distilled water should be added to the maximum level line. All three cells should be filled to same level when seen from side. Water is added from top of battery by removing red cap.

> NOTE: 1. Do not use sulphuric acid.
> 2. Be sure not to impair breather pipe.
> 3. If liquid diminishes extremely fast, check battery charging capacity.

E. Lubrication

Lubricating oils are necessary on parts where two faces contact and move such as rotating or sliding parts in order to decrease the friction and disperse heat from the over-heated parts to prevent excessive wear and scoring. When lubricating oil is not sufficient this not only shortens the machines life, but will result in impeding the overall mechanical performance. This also of course pertains to the SUPER CUB and the major parts must be replaced or replenished with guarranteed high-quality oil at periodical intervals.

(1) Lubricating service where periodical replacement or replenishment is required.

Some parts only require replacement or replenishment of lubricating oils when parts are disassembled for repair or when complete overhaul is performed, and not periodically.

In other words,

Steering Stem Ball Race Cone
Front and Rear Brake Cam
Throttle Grip
Brake Pedal Shaft
} Grease

Steps for Changing Oil	Remarks
① Set vehicle on stand, start engine and warm up oil.	When oil is warm it is easy to change.
② Remove drain bolt on bottom of crankcase. Drain oil.	
③ Insert drain bolt. Pour oil in through oil filler.	
④ After pouring in 0.6 l check to see if oil comes up to oil level (a) with oil guage on cap.	Check in position when cap is not tightened.

> NOTE: 1. Do not exceed standard oil level when putting oil in. Excessive oil will result in oil pumping and insufficient horse power.
> 2. Always change oil at set intervals as oil gets dirty easily.
> 3. Do not use unknown brands of oil.
> 4. Do not use oils that contain water or dust.

(2) Changing of crankcase oil

This should be changed according to Periodical Inspection Chart.

(3) Replenishing of grease

Periodically grease nipples and others.

(a) Greasing Nipples

Grease all places with nipples. Use grease pump. Grease until excessive grease overflows from portion requiring lubrication.

Use "fiber" grease.

NOTE: Replace faulty nipples, which do not accept grease.

(b) Front and Rear Axle Bearings

Replace front and rear wheel bearing grease every 5,000 km (or every 5 months).

Steps for Work	Remarks
① Remove front and rear wheels.	
② Remove bearings by hand.	If tight, lightly tap from inside.
③ Take off old grease and wash bearing with cleaning solvent then dry thoroughly.	
④ Pack bearings with grease, putting some in hub and insert bearings.	Be sure to pack grease so balls are well greased.
⑤ Use "fiber grease".	

NOTE: Be careful not to get any dirt or dust in bearings when removing wheels to repair flats, etc.

(4) Drive chain lubrication

Normally lubrication is done by dropping oil in through peep hole when monthly inspection is performed and to prolong chain life follow the proceeding steps about every 5,000 km (every 5 months).

Lubricating Procedure	Remarks
① Remove chain case cover.	
② Remove drive chain.	
③ Wash drive chain with cleaning solvent thoroughly and dry.	Thorough cleaning is required as chain is always dirty.
④ Melt grease by warming in container and put chain inside container so that grease can penetrate inside roller of chain.	
⑤ Take out chain from container and wipe off excess grease and install.	
⑥ Preferably use "chain grease" or else "gear oil".	

F. Inspection for Tightening of Various Parts

(1) Retightening of bolts and nuts of important parts.

In order to prevent loosening of bolts and nuts caused by vibration and wear, etc., from long use it is necessary to tighten the major parts (see following chart). Use torque wrench and tighten to specified capacity.

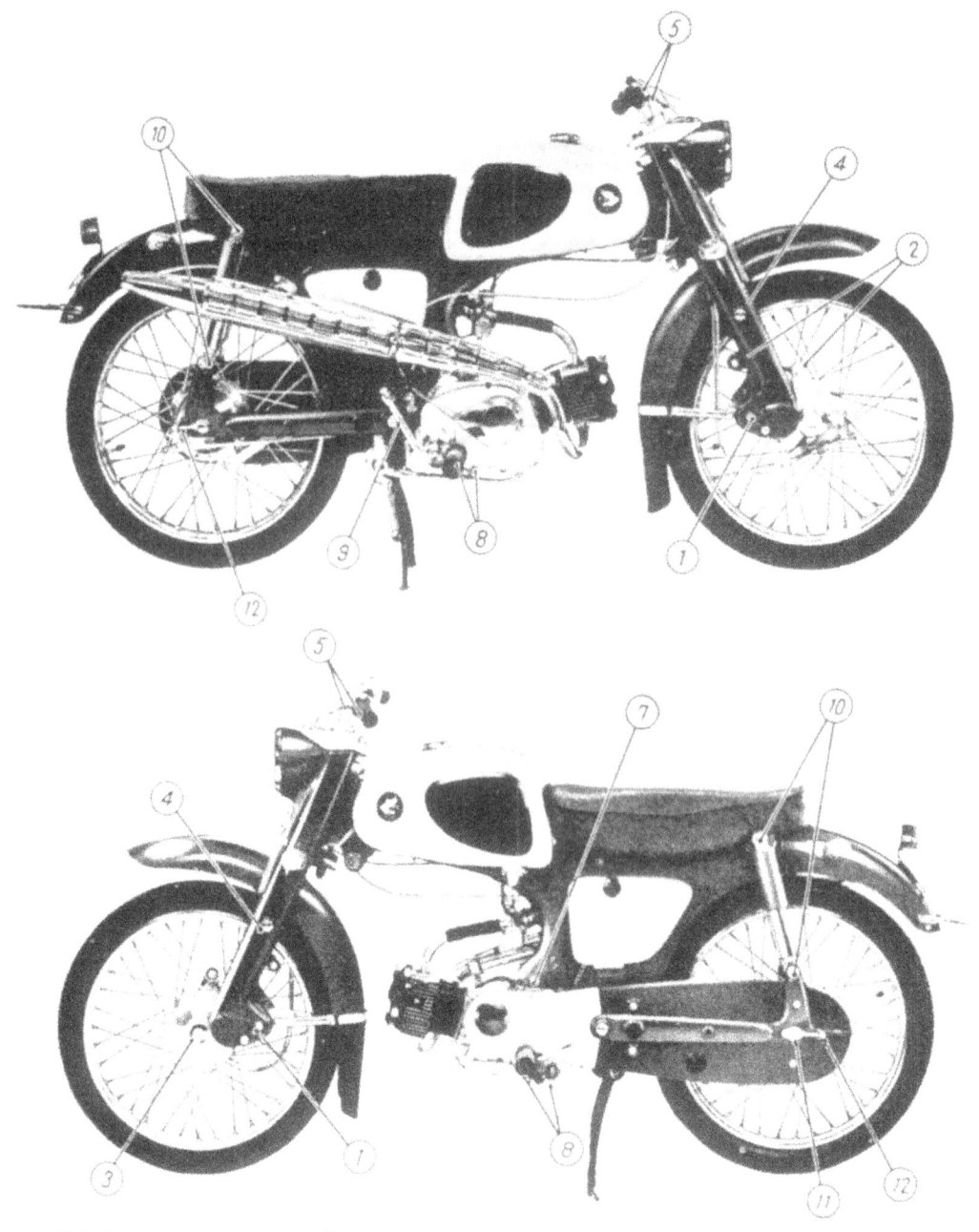

Tightening torque chart.

Parts Name	Tightening Torque			
① Front arm pivot bolt.	3.0	kg-m	20	ft-lb
② Front brake torque link.	3.0	〃	20	〃
③ Front wheel axle nut (1).	3.5~4.5	〃	25~35	〃
④ Front cushion upper bolt (2).	3.0	〃	20	〃
⑤ Steering handle mounting bolts (2).	3.0	〃	20	〃
⑥ Fuel tank mounting bolts (4).	0.7	〃	60	in-lb
⑦ Engine suporting bolts (2).	3.0	〃	20	ft-lb
⑧ Step bar mounting nuts (4).	2.7	〃	18	〃
⑨ Rear fork pivot bolt nut.	6.0	〃	40	〃
⑩ Rear cushion mounting nuts (4).	4.5	〃	30	〃
⑪ Rear wheel axle nut.	3.5~4.5	〃	25~35	〃
Rear cushion sleeve nut.	6.0~6.3	〃	40~50	〃
⑫ Drive chain adjuster nut (2).	0.7	〃	60	in-lb

Fig. 53

(2) Tightening of wheel spokes.

It is necessary to tighten loose spokes periodically or else when vehicle is run with some spokes loose this will affect the rim and the strength of the other spokes. Prescribed period is every 2000 mile (2 month). Check each spoke by turning the nipple, with the wheels off the ground, and tighten any loose spokes to the same amount as others. Use nipple wrench. Check both front and rear wheels.

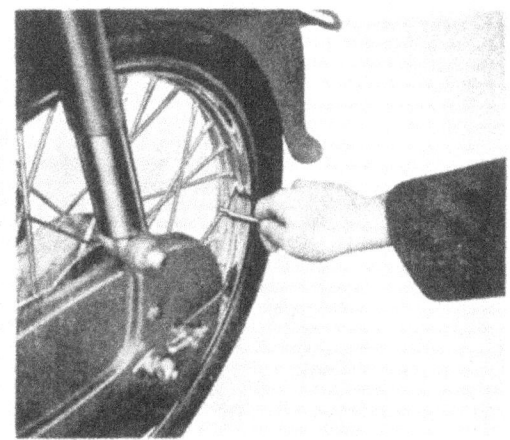

4.2 PERIODIC INSPECTIONS AND MAINTAINANCE

For the protection of the vehicle, perform inspections and maintenance periodically, to prevent troubles from occuring entirely and at the same time do not neglect to take care of vehicle to always keep it in best condition. There is the daily inspection to be performed by the driver every day and the periodic inspections to be performed by the dealer at set intervals.

A. Daily Inspection

The following items should be habitually done by the driver before use every day.

These items should be included and repeated in the periodic inspection and maintained.

(1) Check front and rear tire pressure.
    Front tire   22 psi   Rear tire   28 psi
(2) Check brake appliance and condition of free play.
    Condition of brakes when depressed on or gripped.
        Free Play End of front brake lever   30 - 40 mm (1.2 - 1.6")
                    Top of brake pedal (see p. 41)   20 - 30 mm (0.8 - 1.2")
(3) Check operation of clutch.
    Releasing action
    Slipping action.
(4) Check oil level of crankcase.
    Check condition of oil.
(5) Check fuel level of gasoline tank.
(6) Check horn.
(7) Check headlamp, directional signal lamp, tail lamp, neutral lamp, etc.

B. Periodic Inspections

The following is a chart of contents and time for periodic inspections and maintenances.

MEMO

_____

_____

_____

_____

_____

_____

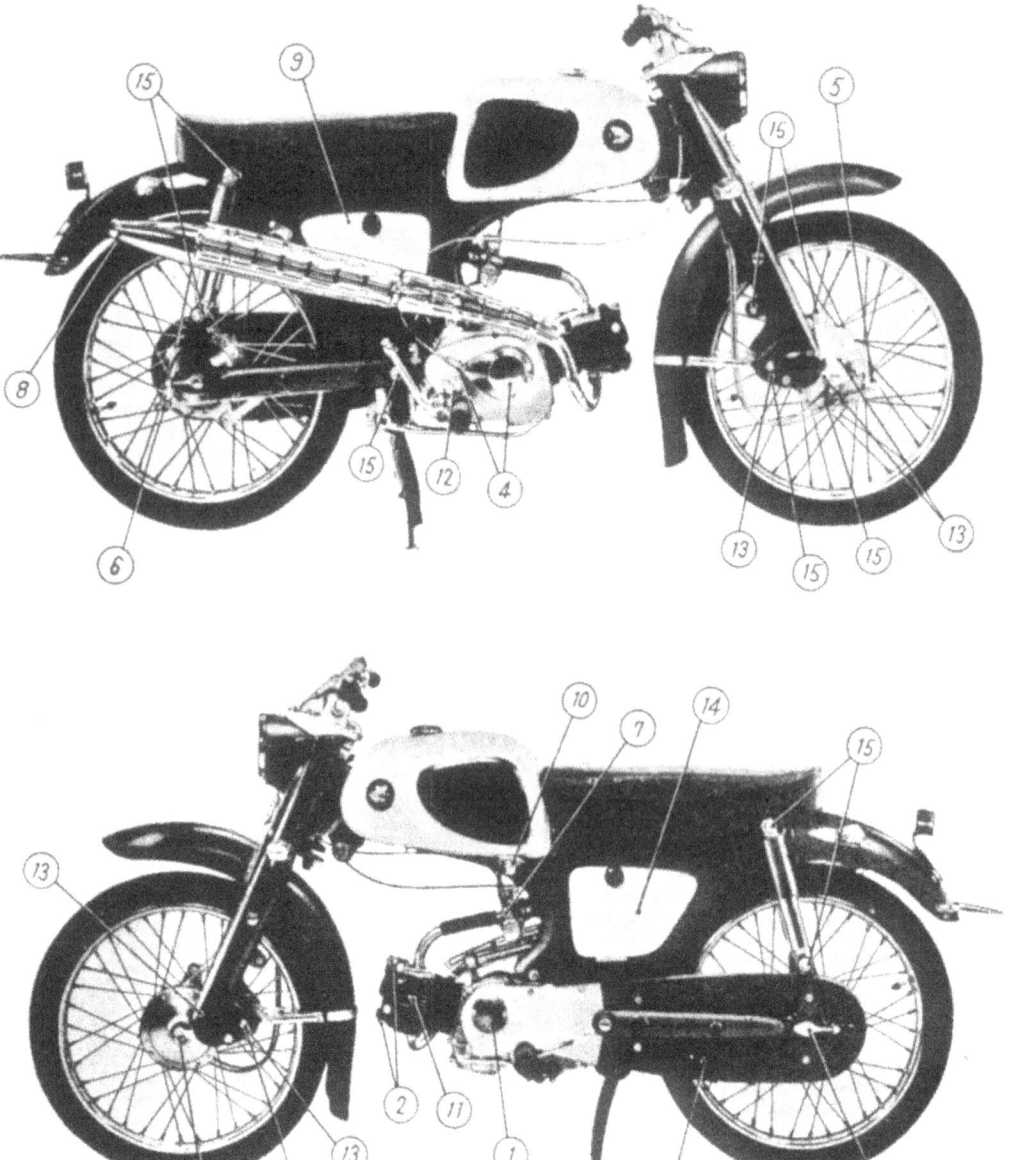

Fig. 55

(1) Adjust timing each 1000 miles
(2) Adjust rocker arms each 500 miles
(3) Adjust rear chain each 500 miles
(4) Adjust clutch each 500 miles
(5) Adjust front brake as needed
(6) Adjust rear brake as needed
(7) Clean carburetor each 2500 miles
(8) Clean muffler or difuser each 2000 miles
(9) Clean air filter each 2000 miles
(10) Clean fuel valve each 1000 miles
(11) Clean and adjust spark plug each 1000 miles
(12) Check oil each 200 mile—change each 1000 miles
(13) Grease fittings
(14) Check battery each 1000 miles
(15) Tighten nut and bolts all the time

4.3 Diagnosis of Troubles

It is important to detect the origin of the trouble when it occurs with the vehicle. The following chart lists the ways and means for best and correct detection of the trouble. As the steps for diagnosis and the probable cause is listed according to the trouble, once the cause is discovered, proper steps for maintenance can be taken.

NOTE: ○ Shows the vehicle with trouble.
        △ Shows the vehicle accomplished remedy.

A. Engine Does Not Start or Difficult to Start.

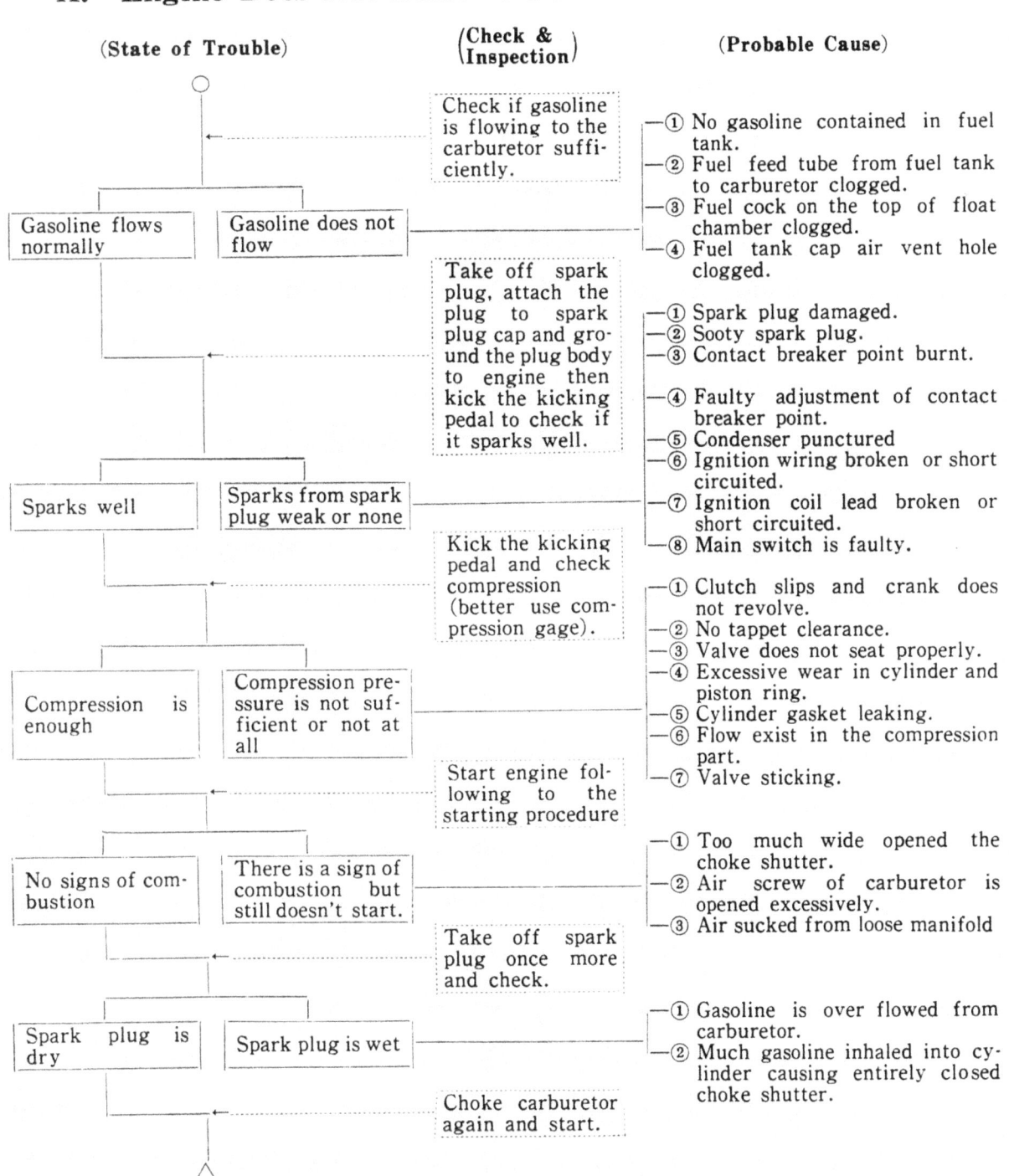

B. Machine Does Not Develop Full Power or Not Make Enough Speed

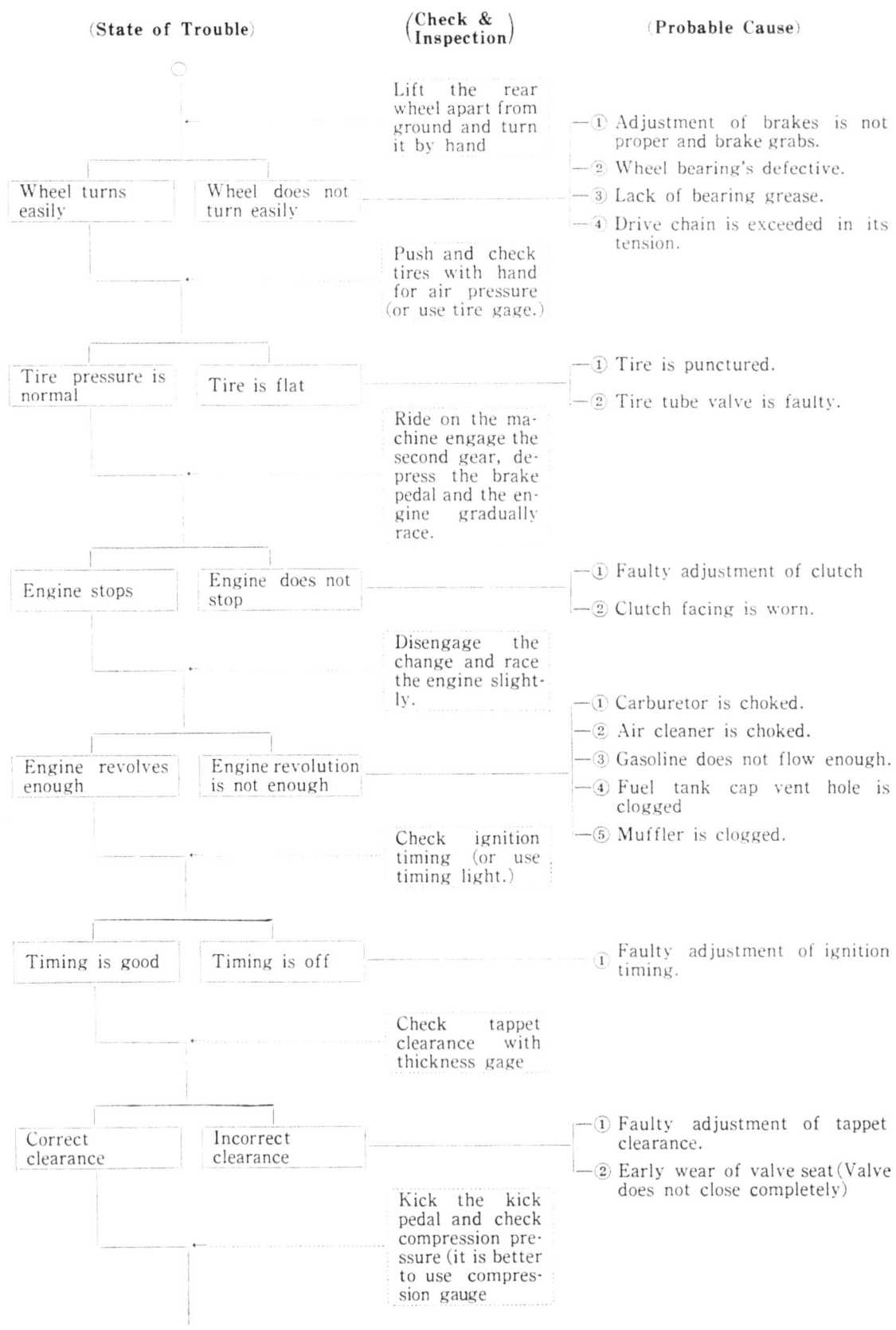

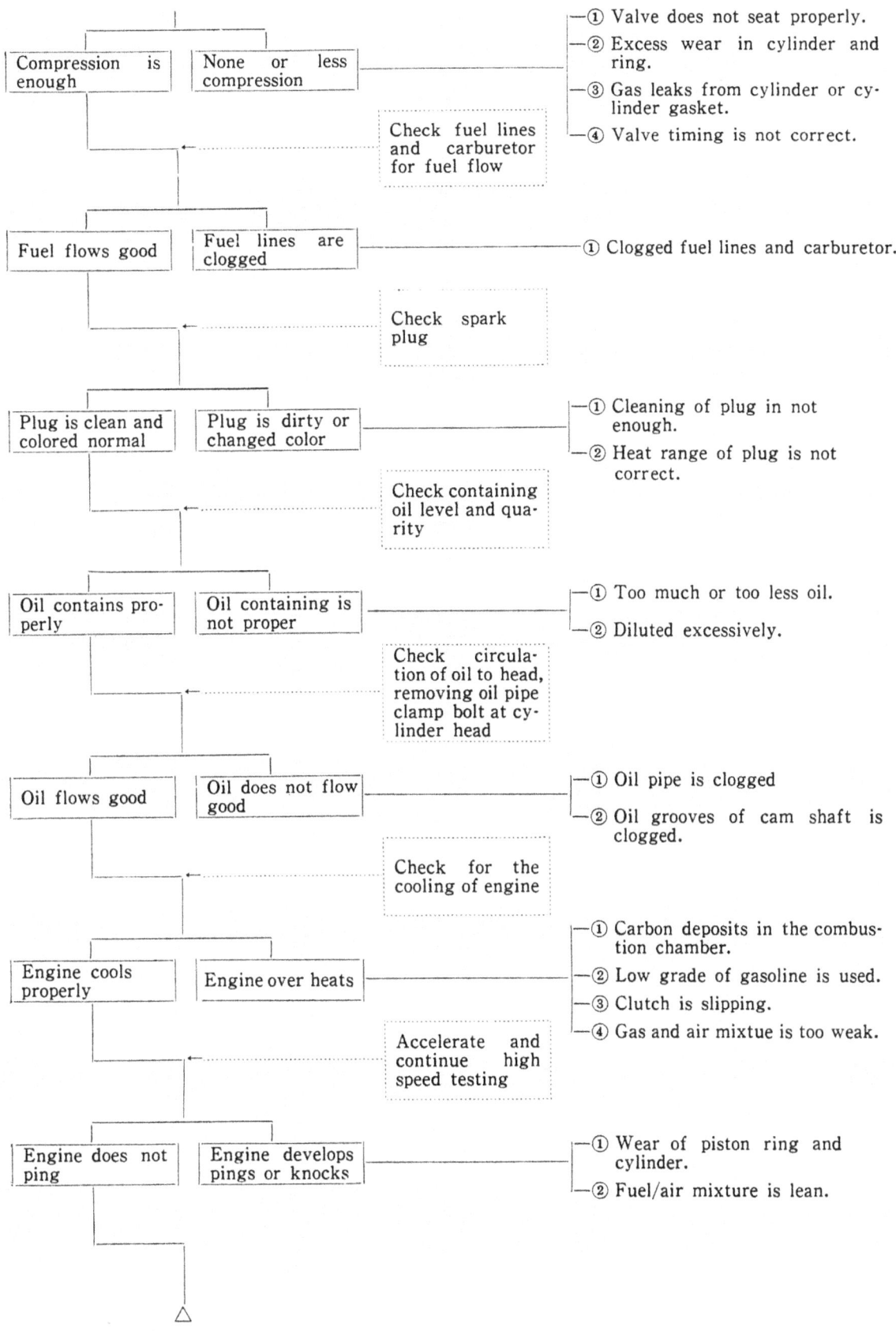

C. Engine Missfires at Idling or Low Speed Running

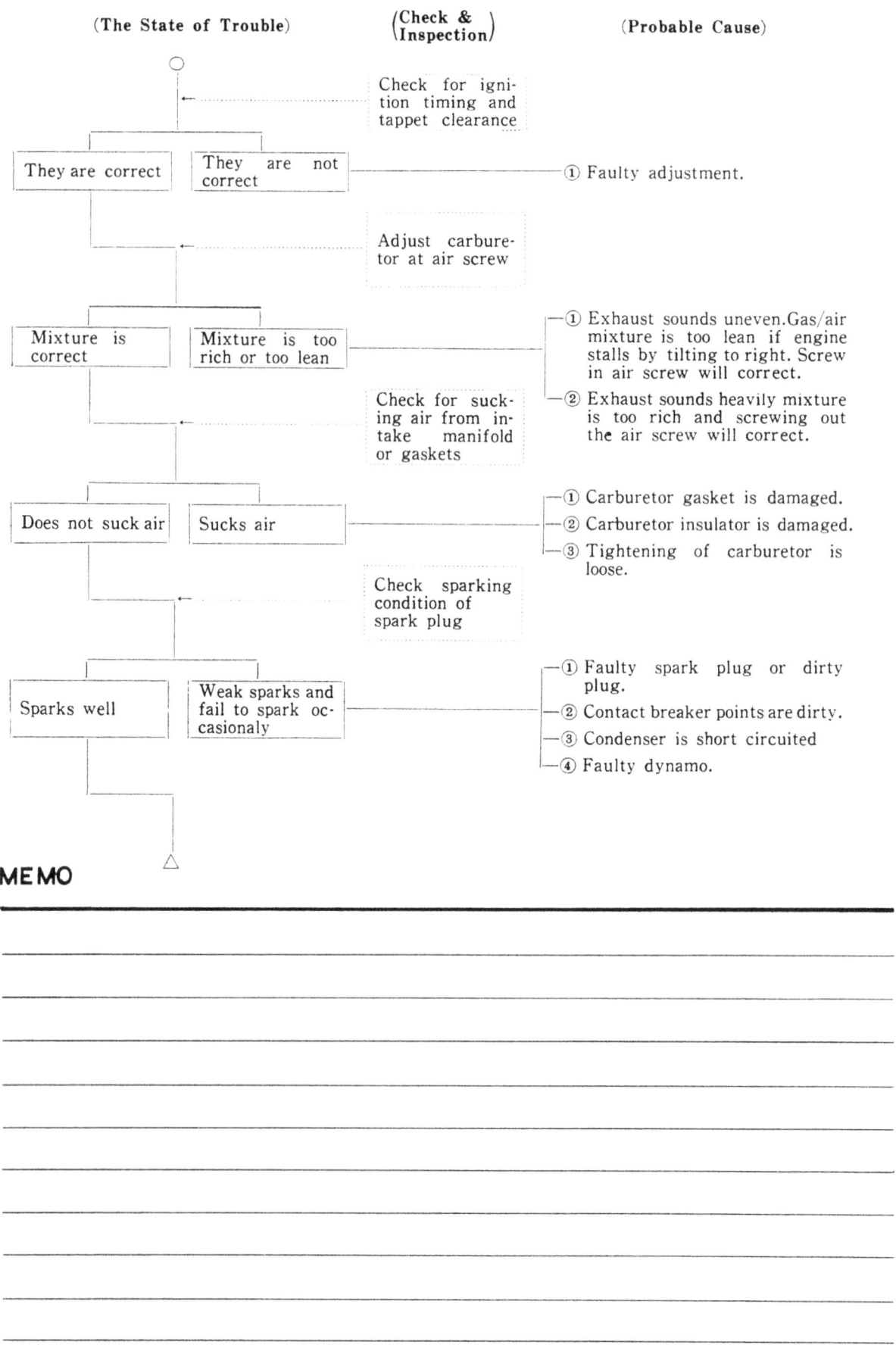

D. Engine Missfires at High Speed.

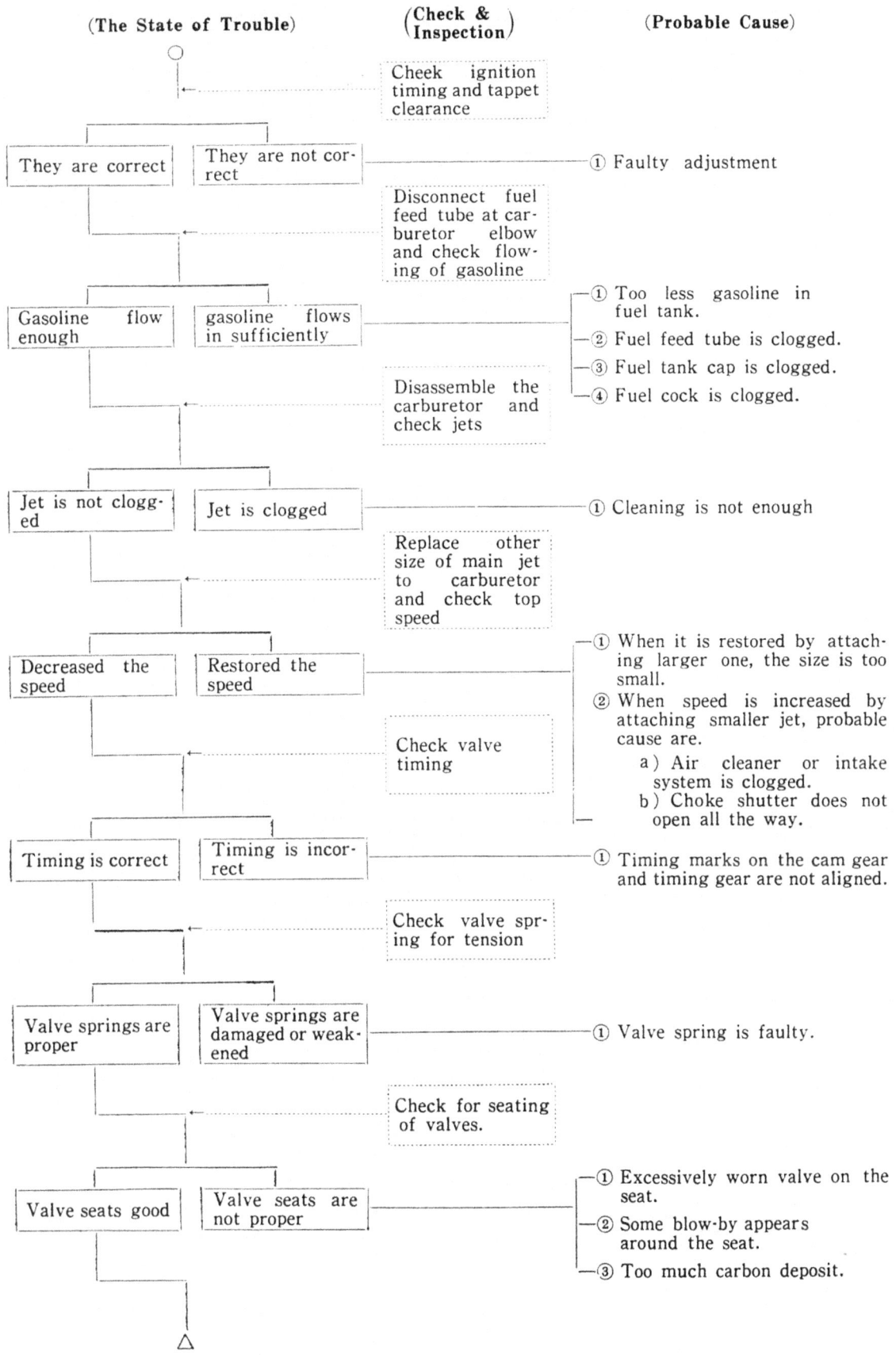

E. Engine Consumes Excess Oil in Combustion Chamber
(Muffler exhaust white or black smoke)

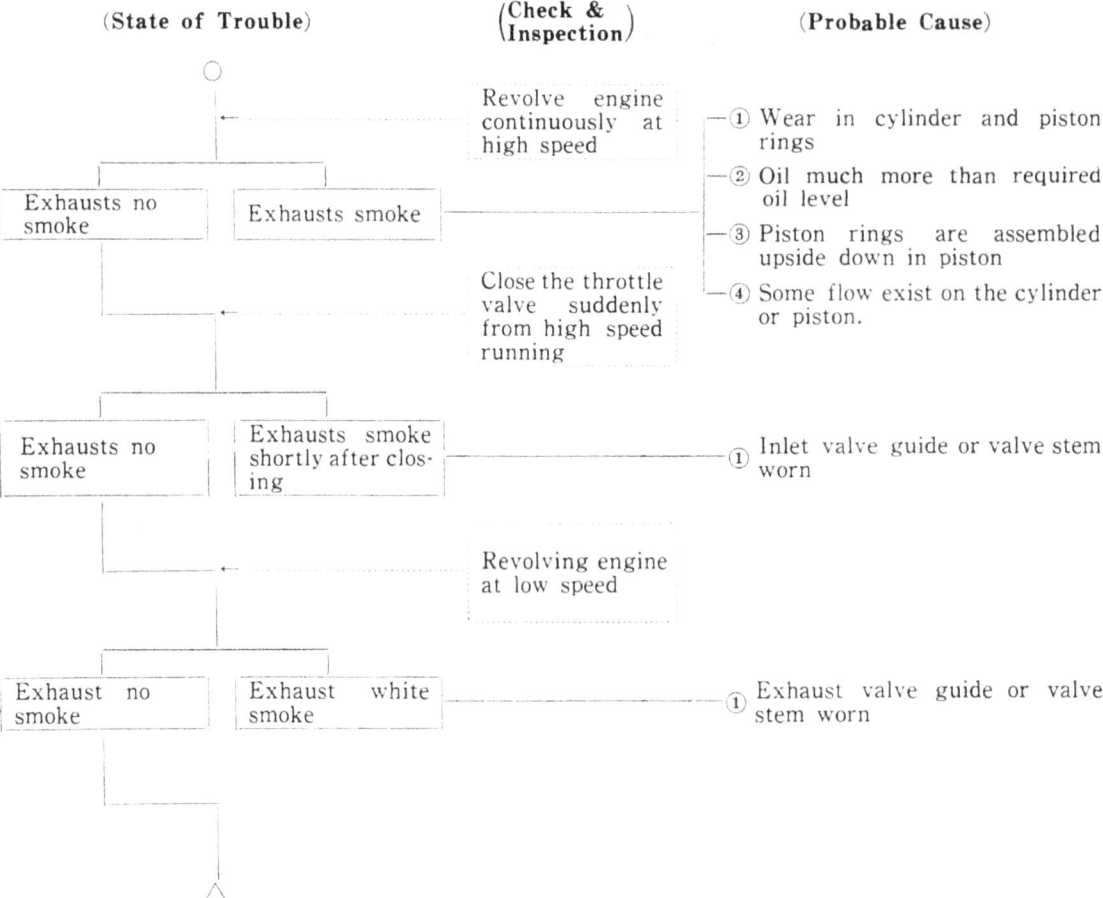

F. Clutch Doesn't Function Properly

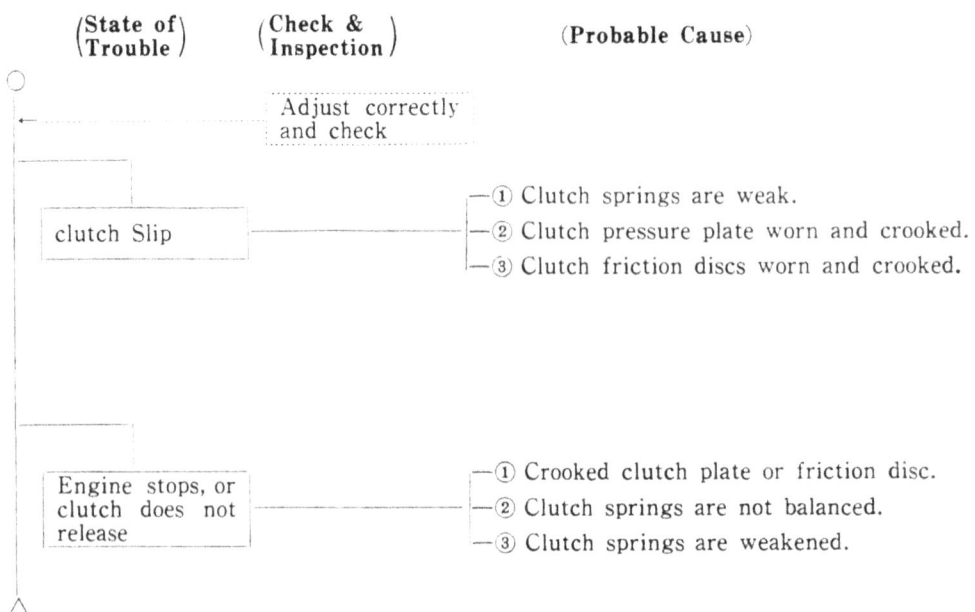

G. Change Does Not Function Properly

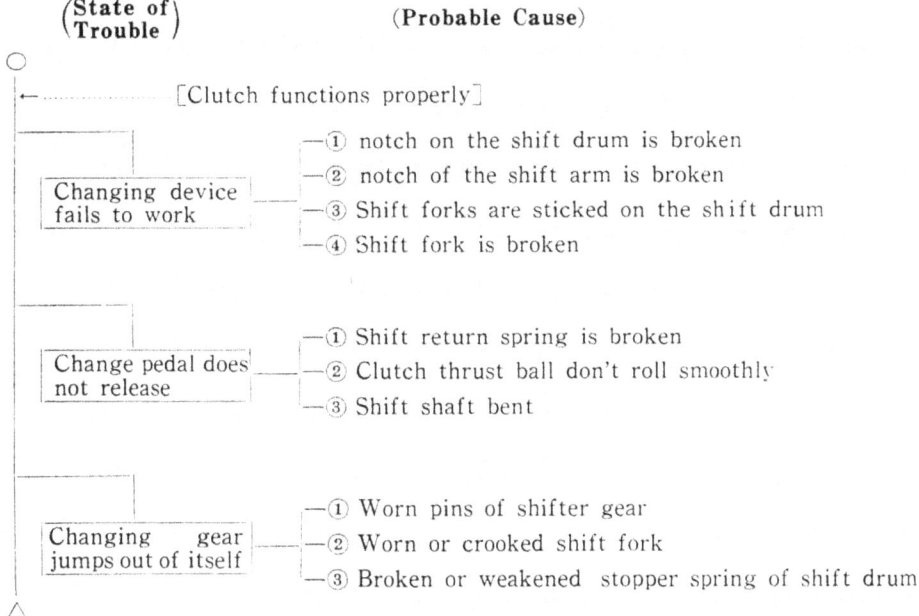

H. Engine Emmits Noise

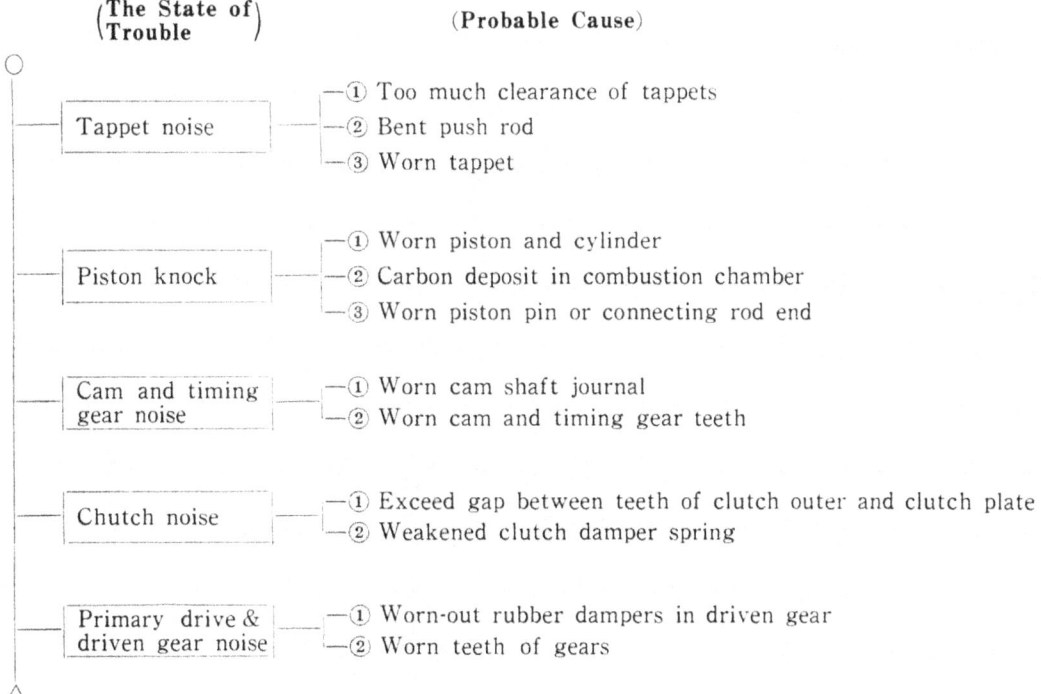

I. Unstable Steering

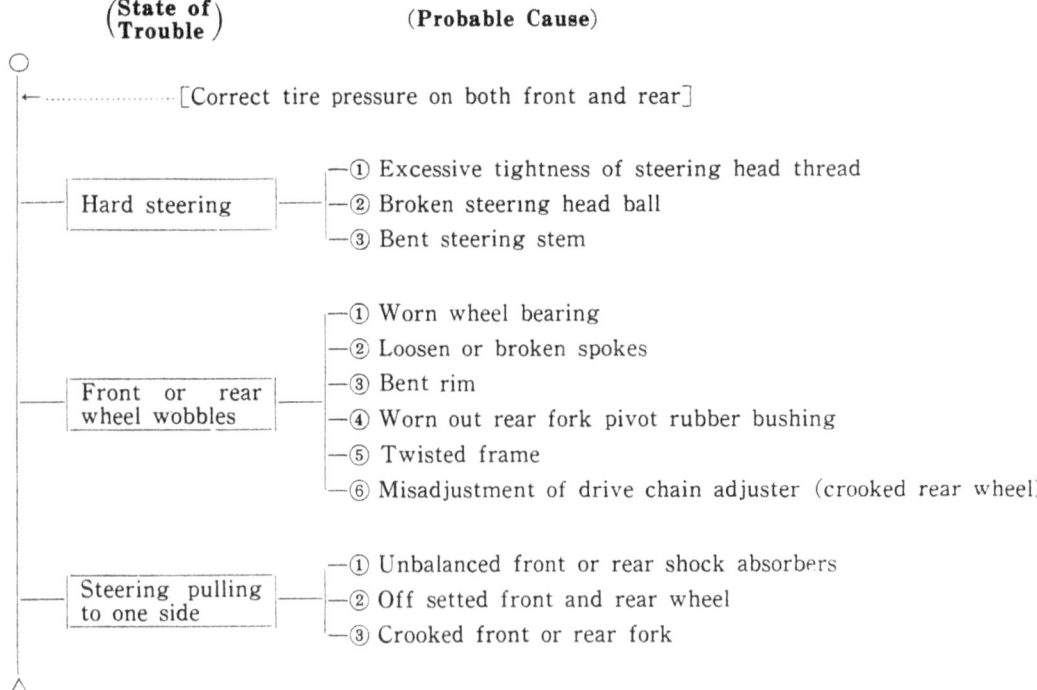

J. Front and Rear Spring and Shock-absorber Function Inaccurately

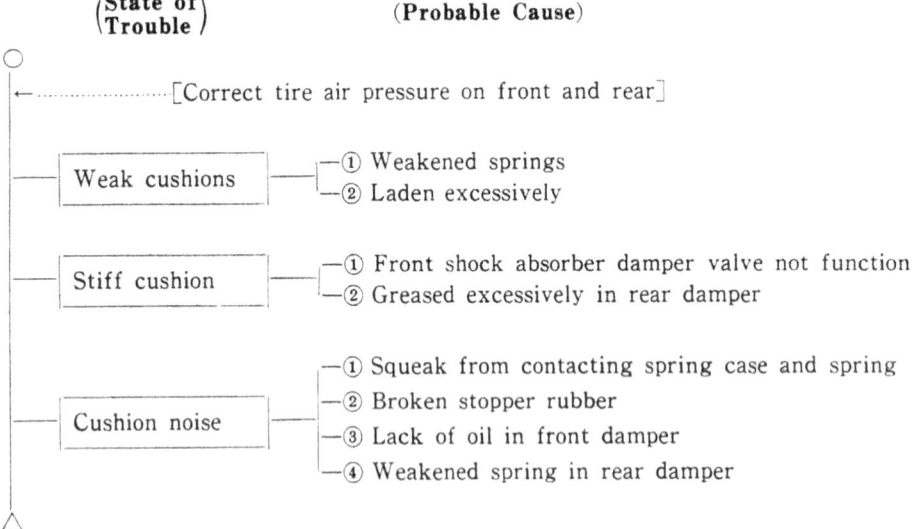

K. Brake Functions Inaccurate

$\begin{pmatrix}\text{State of}\\\text{Trouble}\end{pmatrix}$ (Probable Cause)

- .... [Adjust brakes correctly]

- **Unadjustable**
  - ① Excess wear in brake shoe
  - ② Excess wear in brake shoe cam

- **Make noise when brake's applied**
  - ① Excess wear in brake shoe
  - ② Dirt accumulated arround facing
  - ③ Rough surface of brake drum

- **Brake does not work**
  - ① Front brake wire does not function
  - ② Excessive wear in brake shaft and brake pipe - water or oil on surface of brake.

L. Excess Wear in Drive Chain

$\begin{pmatrix}\text{State of}\\\text{Trouble}\end{pmatrix}$ (Probable Cause)

- **Early in slackening**
  - ① Fail to keep periodical adjustment
  - ② Fail to keep periodical servicing

- **Dust inhale in chain case**
  - ① Defective chain case rubber packing

- **Early in wearing of sprocket**
  - ① Dust in chain case

MEMO

_____
_____
_____
_____
_____
_____
_____
_____
_____

4.4 Maintenance Data & Specifications

A. Maintenance Data

In order to operate the vehicle in best condition and also extend its life it is necessary to perform without fail the preceeding periodic inspections and prevent trouble from occuring from the beginning. Use the following standards to determine whether overhaul is required or not.

	Standard Value	Unavailable Limit	Procedure on Measuring
Compression Pressure	125 lb./in.	90 lb./in.	Use compression gage, check with kick and while engine is warm.
Fuel Consumption	85–90 km/l (210-220 m.p.g.)	50 km/l (140 m.p.g.)	Use fuel consumption gage, test on level road (paved) running with constant speed 30 km/hr (19 mile/hr) in the top gear.
Max. Top Speed	75 km/hr (43 mile/hr)	50 km/hr (35 mile/hr)	Test on a level road, when there is no wind, with full throttle, top gear and the posture with upper half of body leaning forward.
Stopping Ability (distance)	max. 5m (16.5 ft.)	over 10m (33 ft.)	Test on a dry level road (paved), when solo and initial speed is 25km/hr (16 mile/hr), front and rear brake applied at same time.

When interior noise and oil consumption, in other words oil pumping, is excessive determine cause according to diagnosis of trouble means and service.

B. Specifications of Performances

The following chart lists assembly performance specifications and parts size standards, which should be used for reference when performing service.

MEMO

C. Specification of Parts

  (1) Maintenance of common parts.

Even parts not listed in the next chart should always be checked and inspected for the following points and acted upon with proper judgement.

The following is also a standard chart for dealers to determine whether parts are beyond limit of repair.

- (1) Rubber made parts.....Especially oil seal rubber bushing and cushion parts should be replaced when found too old, distorted, damaged and elasticity gone, etc.
- (2) Bearing parts.....Ball, roller, needle bearing, etc., should be replaced when found worn, damaged, movement not smooth, etc.
- (3) Packing, gasket parts.....All should be replaced. Especially when liquid packing is used, clean thoroughly repack and use.
- (4) Replace snap rings, end rings, set rings, etc., that have lost their tension. End ring as a rule should be replaced.
- (5) Replace deformed or damaged bolts, screws, nuts, washers, etc.
- (6) Only use genuine HONDA parts when newly installing (purchased through authorized HONDA dealers).

  (2) Definition of words used in chart.

STANDARD VALUE.....This indicates the manufacturer's standard size or the standard size after newly assembling or adjusting and shows the size-limit of completed part or the permissable limit of adjustment.

REPAIRING LIMIT.....Unusable wear limit of parts requiring correction or replacement, function-wise.

REMARKS.....Additional instructions on measuring or servicing.

ITEMS.....Items to be inspected, service-wise.

  (3) Units in Chart.

Unmarked numbers are mm unit and inch unit in parenthesis, and others according to the unit indicated.

MEMO

	Item	Standard	Repairing Limit	Remarks
1. Cylinder & Cylinder Head Block	Cylinder bore	40.0–40.01mm (1.575–1.576)	max. 40.1mm (1.580)	
	Max. Cylinder out of round	0.01 (0.0004)	max. 0.05(0.002)	
	Cylinder out of taper	0.01 (0.0004)	max. 0.05(0.002)	
	Height of cylinder	63.2–63.4 (2.49–2.497)	min. 63.1 (2.485)	
2. Crankshaft (include piston connecting rod)	Piston top diameter	39.63–39.68 (1.561–1.563)		
	Piston skirt diameter	39.98–40.0 (1.575–1.930)		Thrust face
	Width of piston ring groove			
	Top and second	1.51–1.53 (0.059–0.06)	max. 1.6 (0.063)	Replace
	Oil	3.51–3.53 (0.138–0.139)	max. 3.6 (0.141)	
	Min. clearance of piston to cylinder	0.01–0.03 (0.0005–0.001)	max. 0.14 (0.005)	Rebore
	Thickness of piston rings Top and second	1.47–1.49 (0.057–0.058)	min. 1.40 (0.055)	
	Oil	2.480–2.495	min. 2.40 (0.133)	
	Piston ring end gap	0.01–0.3 (0.003–0.01)	max. 1.0 (0.039)	
	Piston and ring oversize	0.25, 0.50, 0.75 (0.009, 0.019, 0.029)		
	Diameter of connecting rod small end	13.02–13.05 (0.512–0.514)	max. 13.1 (0.516)	
	Clearance of piston pin to connecting rod	0.03–0.05 (0.016–0.049) (0.0015–0.001)	max. 0.08 (0.516)	
	Diameter of connecting rod large end	26.09–26.1 (1.027–1.028)	max. 26.2 (1.032)	
	Radial play of connecting rod	0.006–0.03 (0.0002–0.001)	max. 0.01 (0.0003)	
	Axis play of connecting rod	0.1–0.35 (0.003–0.013)	max. 1.0 (0.039)	
	Diameter of R.L. crankshaft	16.99–17.0 (0.6694–0.6698)	max. 16.9 (0.665)	
	Crankshaft run-out	0.03 (0.001)	max. 0.3 (0.011)	
3. Cam and Valve	Diameter of valve stem			
	Ex.	5.435–5.445 (0.2143–0.2147)	min. 5.40 (0.212)	
	In.	5.46–5.47 (0.2151–0.2155)	min. 5.42 (0.213)	
	Valve seat angle	45 degrees		In. & ex.
	Clearance of valve stem to guide			
	Ex.	0.06–0.08 (0.002–0.003)	max. 0.1 (0.003)	
	In.	0.04–0.06 (0.0015–0.002)	max. 0.1 (0.003)	

	Item	Standard	Repairing Limit	Remarks
3. Cam and Valve	Valve spring compression			
	Outer	6.3–6.9kg	min. 5.4	at 23.5mm (0.925") test length.
	Inner	2.6–2.9kg (5.733–6.394 lb.)	min. 2.2 (0.086 lb.)	at 22.5mm (0.886")
	Diameter of cam shaft journal			
	Large end	30.95–30.98 (1.2194–1.2206)	min. 30.9 (1.217)	
	Small end	18.96–18.98 (0.7470–07.478)	min. 18.9 (0.744)	
	Height of cam	24.5	min. 23.0	
4. Clutch	Clutch center guide			
	Outside diameter	19.94–19.96 (0.7856–0.786)	min. 19.55 (0.770)	
	Inner diameter	17.0–17.01 (0.6968–0.670)	min. 17.15 (0.675)	
	Friction disc thickness	3.5–2.8	min. 2.3 (0.090)	
	Clutch spring free length	25.2	min. 24.00	Replace
5. Transmission and Others	Diameter of main shaft	13.91–13.98 (0.548–0.550)	min. 13.8 (0.531)	
	Diameter of counter shaft	16.98–16.99 (0.6690–0.6694)	min. 16.95 (0.630)	
	Shift drum – Large end	41.95–41.97 (1.652–1.653)	min. 41.9 (1.650)	
	Small end	11.97–11.98 (0.4716–0.4720)	min. 11.9 (0.468)	
6. Frame	Stroke of front cushion	36.0 (1.418)		Containing 9.5cc of No. 60 spindle oil
	Free length of front cushion spring	122.5 (4.826)	min. 117 (4.609)	Replace
	Stroke of rear cushion	63.8 (2.513)		Shock absorb with damper spring
	Free length of rear cushion spring	211.00	min. 206	
	Thickness of brake lining (front and rear)	3.5 (0.137)	min. 2.0 (0.078)	
	Diameter of brake drum (front and rear)	119.8–120.2 (4.720–4.735)	max. 123 (4.836)	
	Run-out of wheel rim (front and rear)	0–1.0 (0–0.039)	max. 3.0 (0.118)	

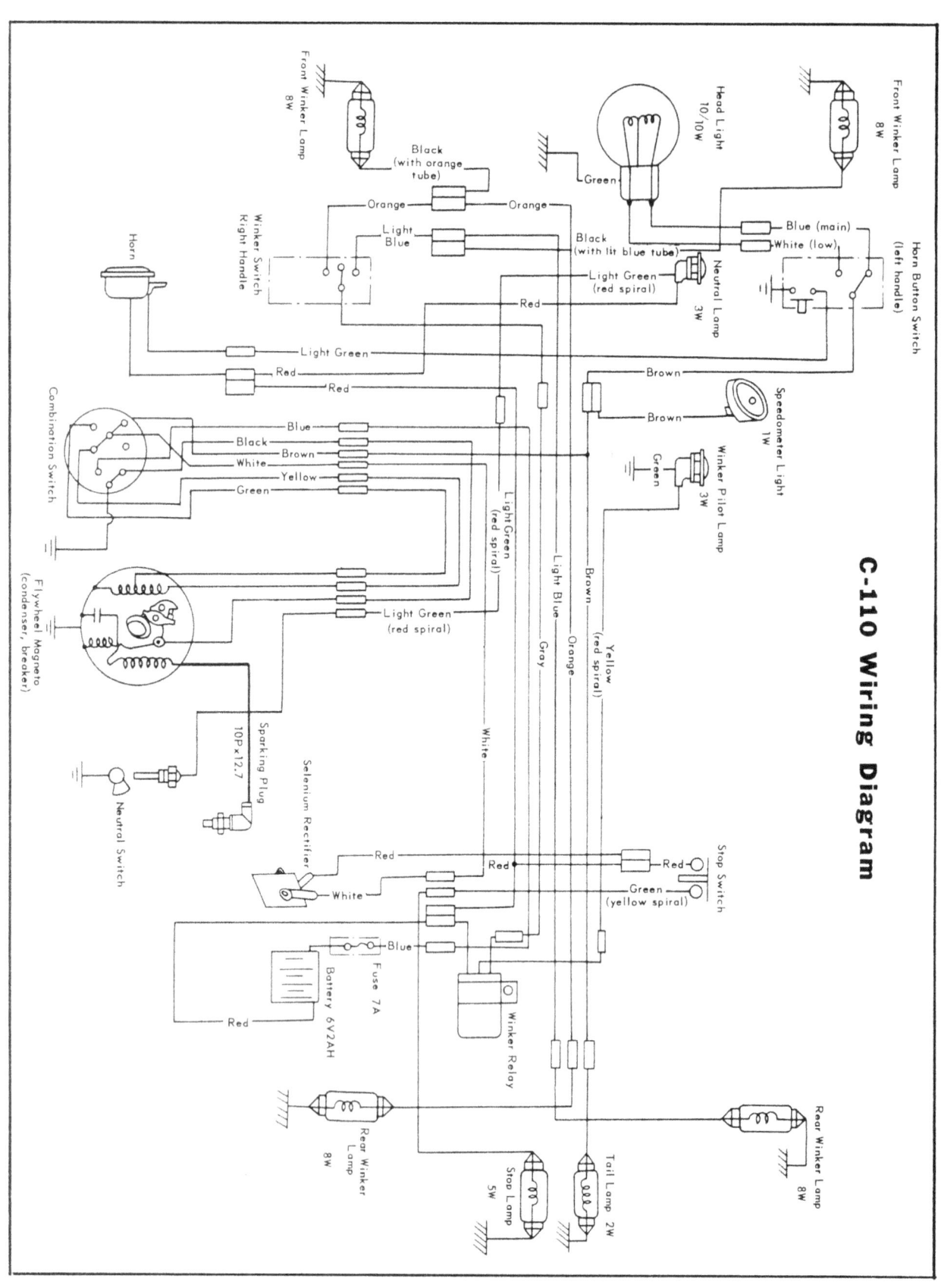

A SAMPLE LIST OF OTHER BOOKS AVAILABLE FROM

www.VelocePress.com

PLEASE CHECK OUR WEBSITE FOR THE MOST UP-TO-DATE INFORMATION

MOTORCYCLE WORKSHOP MANUALS, MAINTENANCE & TECHNICAL TITLES

ARIEL WORKSHOP MANUAL 1933-1951
BMW FACTORY WORKSHOP MANUAL R26 R27 (1956-1967)
BMW FACTORY WSM R50 R50S R60 R69S R50US R60US R69US (1955-1969)
BSA SERVICE & REPAIR ALL PRE-WAR MODELS TO 1939, SV & OHV 150cc TO 1,000cc
DUCATI FACTORY WORKSHOP MANUAL SINGLE CYLINDER NARROW CASE OHC ENGINES 160cc, 250cc, 350cc - MONZA JUNIOR, MONZA, 250GT, MARK 3, MACH 1, MOTOCROSS & SEBRING
HONDA FACTORY WORKSHOP MANUAL 250cc TO 305cc C/CS/CB 72 & 77 SERIES 1960-1969
HONDA FACTORY WORKSHOP MANUAL 125cc TO 150cc C/CS/CB/CA 92 & 95 SERIES 1959-1966
HONDA FACTORY WORKSHOP MANUAL 50cc C110 (1962-1969)
HONDA SERVICE & REPAIR 50cc TO 305cc C100, C102, MONKEY BIKE, CE 105H TRIALS BIKE, C110, C114, C92, CB92, BENLEY, C72, CB72, C77 & CB77
NORTON FACTORY WORKSHOP MANUAL 1957-1970
NORTON WORKSHOP MANUAL 1932-1939
ROYAL ENFIELD 736cc INTERCEPTOR & ENFIELD INDIAN CHIEF
SUZUKI T10 FACTORY WORKSHOP MANUAL 250cc 1963-1967
SUZUKI T20 & T200 FACTORY WORKSHOP MANUAL 200cc X-5 INVADER & STING RAY SCRAMBLER, 250cc X-6 HUSTLER 1965-1969
TRIUMPH FACTORY WORKSHOP MANUAL NO. 11 (1945-1955)
TRIUMPH WORKSHOP MANUAL 1935-1939
TRIUMPH WORKSHOP MANUAL 1937-1951
VESPA SERVICE & REPAIR ALL MODELS 125cc & 150cc 1951-1961
VINCENT SERVICE & REPAIR 1935-1955

CLASSIC AUTO TITLES & REFERENCE BOOKS

ABARTH BUYERS GUIDE
CARRERA PANAMERICANA 1950 ~ THE STORY OF THE 1950 MEXICAN ROAD RACE
DIALED IN ~ THE JAN OPPERMAN STORY
FERRARI 308 SERIES BUYER'S AND OWNER'S GUIDE
FERRARI BERLINETTA LUSSO
FERRARI BROCHURES & SALES LITERATURE 1946-1967
FERRARI SERIAL NUMBERS PART I ~ STREET CARS TO SERIAL # 21399 (1948-1977)
FERRARI SERIAL NUMBERS PART II ~ RACE CARS TO SERIAL # 1050 (1948-1973)
FERRARI SPYDER CALIFORNIA
IF HEMINGWAY HAD WRITTEN A RACING NOVEL ~ THE BEST OF MOTOR RACING FICTION 1950-2000
LE MANS 24 ~ WHAT THE MOVIE COULD HAVE BEEN
MASERATI BROCHURES AND SALES LITERATURE ~ POSTWAR THROUGH INLINE 6 CYLINDER CARS

All VelocePress titles are available through your local independent bookseller, Amazon.com, or they may be purchased directly through our website at www.VelocePress.com. Wholesale customers may also purchase directly from us or from the Ingram Book Group.

A SAMPLE LIST OF OTHER BOOKS AVAILABLE FROM

www.VelocePress.com

PLEASE CHECK OUR WEBSITE FOR THE MOST UP-TO-DATE INFORMATION

AUTOBOOKS SERIES OF WORKSHOP MANUALS

ALFA ROMEO GIULIA 1750, 2000 1962-1978 WORKSHOP MANUAL
AUSTIN HEALEY SPRITE, MG MIDGET 1958-1980 WORKSHOP MANUAL
BMW 1600 1966-1973 WORKSHOP MANUAL
FIAT 1100, 1100D, 1100R & 1200 1957-1969 WORKSHOP MANUAL
FIAT 124 1966-1974 WORKSHOP MANUAL
FIAT 124 SPORT 1966-1975 WORKSHOP MANUAL
FIAT 125 & 125 SPECIAL 1967-1973 WORKSHOP MANUAL
FIAT 126, 126L, 126DV, 126/650 & 126/650DV 1972-1982 WORKSHOP MANUAL
FIAT 127 SALOON, SPECIAL & SPORT, 900, 1050 1971-1981 WORKSHOP MANUAL
FIAT 128 1969-1982 WORKSHOP MANUAL
FIAT 1300, 1500 1961-1967 WORKSHOP MANUAL
FIAT 131 MIRAFIORI 1975-1982 WORKSHOP MANUAL
FIAT 132 1972-1982 WORKSHOP MANUAL
FIAT 500 1957-1973 WORKSHOP MANUAL
FIAT 600, 600D & MULTIPLA 1955-1969 WORKSHOP MANUAL
FIAT 850 1964-1972 WORKSHOP MANUAL
JAGUAR E-TYPE 1961-1972 WORKSHOP MANUAL
JAGUAR MK 1, 2 1955-1969 WORKSHOP MANUAL
JAGUAR S TYPE, 420 1963-1968 WORKSHOP MANUAL
JAGUAR XK 120, 140, 150 MK 7, 8, 9 1948-1961 WORKSHOP MANUAL
LAND ROVER 1, 2 1948-1961 WORKSHOP MANUAL
MERCEDES-BENZ 190 1959-1968 WORKSHOP MANUAL
MERCDEDS-BENZ 220/8 1968-1972 WORKSHOP MANUAL
MERCEDES-BENZ 230 1963-1968 WORKSHOP MANUAL
MERCEDES-BENZ 250 1968-1972 WORKSHOP MANUAL
MG MIDGET TA-TF 1936-1955 WORKSHOP MANUAL
MINI 1959-1980 WORKSHOP MANUAL
MORRIS MINOR 1952-1971 WORKSHOP MANUAL
PEUGEOT 404 1960-1975 WORKSHOP MANUAL
PORSCHE 911 1964-1969 WORKSHOP MANUAL
PORSCHE 911 1970-1977 WORKSHOP MANUAL
RENAULT 8, 10, 1100 1962-1971 WORKSHOP MANUAL
RENAULT 16 1965-1979 WORKSHOP MANUAL
ROVER 3500, 3500S 1968-1976 WORKSHOP MANUAL
SUNBEAM RAPIER, ALPINE 1955-1965 WORKSHOP MANUAL
TRIUMPH SPITFIRE, GT6, VITESSE 1962-1968 WORKSHOP MANUAL
TRIUMPH TR2, TR3, TR3A 1952-1962 WORKSHOP MANUAL
TRIUMPH TR4, TR4A 1961-1967 WORKSHOP MANUAL
VOLKSWAGEN BEETLE 1968-1977 WORKSHOP MANUAL

All VelocePress titles are available through your local independent bookseller, Amazon.com, or they may be purchased directly through our website at www.VelocePress.com. Wholesale customers may also purchase directly from us or from the Ingram Book Group.

A SAMPLE LIST OF OTHER BOOKS AVAILABLE FROM

www.VelocePress.com

PLEASE CHECK OUR WEBSITE FOR THE MOST UP-TO-DATE INFORMATION

OTHER WORKSHOP MANUALS, MAINTENANCE & TECHNICAL TITLES

AUSTIN HEALEY SIX CYLINDER CARS 1956-1968
BMW ISETTA FACTORY REPAIR MANUAL
FERRARI 250/GT SERVICE AND MAINTENANCE
FERRARI GUIDE TO PERFORMANCE
FERRARI OPERATING, MAINTENANCE & SERVICE HANDBOOKS 1948-1963
FERRARI OWNER'S HANDBOOK
FERRARI TUNING TIPS & MAINTENANCE TECHNIQUES
MASERATI OWNER'S HANDBOOK
OBERT'S FIAT GUIDE
PERFORMANCE TUNING THE SUNBEAM TIGER
PORSCHE 356 SERVICE AND MAINTENANCE MANUAL 1948-1965
PORSCHE 912 WORKSHOP MANUAL
SOUPING THE VOLKSWAGEN IMPROVING THE PERFORMANCE OF YOUR VW
TRIUMPH TR2, TR3 & TR4 WORKSHOP MANUAL
VOLVO ALL MODELS 1944-1968 WORKSHOP MANUAL

BROOKLANDS ROAD TEST PORTFOLIOS

FIAT DINO 1968-1973
MV AGUSTA F4 750 & 1000 1997-2007
JAGUAR MK1 & MK2 1955-1969
LOTUS CORTINA 1963-1970
FIAT 500 1936-1972
FERRARI ROAD CARS 1946-1956

All VelocePress titles are available through your local independent bookseller, Amazon.com, or they may be purchased directly through our website at www.VelocePress.com. Wholesale customers may also purchase directly from us or from the Ingram Book Group.

www.ingramcontent.com/pod-product-compliance
Lightning Source LLC
Chambersburg PA
CBHW081926170426
43200CB00014B/2843